'You have to dance with somebody else to
recognize who you are'
Heinz von Foerster

STAFFORD BEER

A PERSONAL MEMOIR

DAVID WHITTAKER

wavestone
press

This book is dedicated to my wife Penny and daughter Alice
– frolicsome partners in the dance of life.

Stafford Beer: A Personal Memoir
ISBN: 0954519418
Wavestone Press
6 Rochester Place, Charlbury, Oxon OX7 3SF,
Tel. 01608-811858
Email: books@whithew.freeserve.co.uk
www.wavestonepress.co.uk
All material Copyright © David Whittaker 2003 except:
Stafford Beer Letters © Stafford Beer Estate 2003
Brian Eno Interview and Photo © Brian Eno 2003
Robert Fripp Letters © Robert Fripp 2003

ACKNOWLEDGEMENTS

I am very grateful to the Beer family and Allenna Leonard for their support, encouragement and trust. Especially Simon for facilitating a visit to Cwarel Isaf. I spent three days there in late August, alone, working on this book. It was a strange experience placing the letters back on Stafford's desk where so many of them had been written over the previous two decades.

Vanilla Beer's daily e-mails provided a virtual chinwag on the man himself.

Allenna made helpful comments on an early draft.

Brian Eno gave me some thoughtful quality time with his reminiscences. It is a particular pleasure for me to bring Brian and Stafford together between these covers as both have, in different ways, acted as mentors.

Thanks to Robert Fripp for permission to use two letters.

The shape of this book owes much to Keith Rigley's highly focussed and refined mouse-clicking eye. Cheers again chap!

A fortuitous meeting with Stafford's neighbour Gareth Jones resulted in a useful Welsh lesson (page 29). *Iechyd da!*

Front endpaper: The beech-lined road to Cwarel Isaf
Rear endpaper: Bust of Stafford outside the cottage by Vanilla

50 copies of this book have been signed and numbered for subscribers (I appreciate your patience and faith!).

Printed by Information Press, Eynsham, Oxon

CONTENTS

INTRODUCTION:
THE CYBERNETICS OF FRIENDSHIP

The date: October 11, 2002. The venue: The Royal Society of Arts, London. The occasion: A Celebration of the Life of Stafford Beer who died on August 25.
To be more precise, about a hundred people are gathered in the vaults. Stafford's partner Allenna Leonard gives a moving talk about his final difficult illness. We listen to a favourite song: a poem of Antonio Machado set to music. Allenna then reads Stafford's translation.

This is followed by a variety of people from all walks of life talking about their relationship with Stafford (this didn't include his large family). I read a 'letter' to him (Appendix 1). Throughout the evening we laugh and we cry. The point is that there is such a diversity. Stafford was many things to many people. I'm reminded of a quote from the poet Walt Whitman (who Stafford came to resemble), 'You say I contradict myself? Very well, I contradict myself – I am large, I contain multitudes'. This is not to say that Stafford contradicted himself (he wouldn't be human if he didn't), but that he was a kind of one-man pluralist society. He magnanimously met the various needs of people on many levels. In fact we'll never know how many. There must be countless platoons of students going back decades; professional colleagues from industry, publishing, academia and management; government officials; artists and writers; yoga students; and just people from day to day activity (especially bar staff). He engaged heartily with people whoever and wherever they were.

I'm not sure where I fit here (Stafford hated categorisation): I was a dealer in second-hand books who was fascinated by his ideas. I have no academic background and no academic agenda to pursue, which I think appealed to him ('autodidact' was the first big word I taught myself). I have been, and still am, a hedonistic reader: I read only for pleasure and roam about freely along the spacious corridors constructed by the human imagination, whether we label them myth, science, philosophy, religion, aesthetics or just plain nonsense. What is essential is a sense of play and the latin word 'ludus' is important here. The pursuit of knowledge is a kind of a game and Stafford had an alert ludic mind. We developed a good cybernetic friendship in that it was a dynamic exchange and interaction over time, from which we both learned and increased each other's options for understanding. The books and papers remain for us all to turn to and I for one am still learning from them.

After Stafford died I rummaged through various boxes of stuff in the loft and found about 60 letters from him. The idea came to me that they could be placed within an interesting chronological narrative and maybe other people might even find it a good read, especially if they knew Stafford. There have been moments compiling this book when I have wondered whether this is simply an act of self-indulgence; on a certain level it is, as all acts, including altruism, can be taken as gratification of some need. But on a broader level I also hope it is an act of sharing. Stafford was the most compassionate and courageous man I've met and I'd like the world to know that. I feel I received far more than I gave, so this is a slightly belated homage of gratitude that I deem I owe him. I have no doubt that there are more memoirs waiting out there, similar to this one (or even quite different), that could be assembled. Perhaps this will start a trend. But this little book is merely a thread (a recurring metaphor) from a richly patterned, self-weaving tapestry known to the world as Stafford Beer.

STAFFORD BEER:
A PERSONAL MEMOIR

I first became aware of Stafford Beer – not in some learned academic publication such as *Journal of Operational Research*, *Systems Practice* or *Kybernetes*
– but in *New Musical Express* a weekly pop newspaper. The date was December
3rd 1977 (I still have the issue) and it included a lengthy interview with Brian
Eno. Eno had been a founder member of the band Roxy Music and had subsequently embarked on a bold and innovative solo career with occasional
collaborations (including, at this time, with David Bowie). I had been a fan since
1972 and found that his interviews never failed to inform and stimulate. In this
instance he cited a book, *Brain of the Firm*, by Beer and made it clear that this
was an important influence on his music making. There was also a reference to
an article he'd written for *Studio International* (Nov./Dec. 1976): *Organising and
Generating Variety in the Arts* (Eno opens this piece with the provocative decla-
ration: 'A musical score is a statement about organization; it is a set of devices
for organizing behaviour towards producing sounds.'). I set about searching for
both these items. The *Studio* was fairly easy to get, but I was told *Brain* was out
of print. In the article Eno gave a more detailed account of cybernetics and
Beer's work which whetted my appetite to find out more. A few months later I
chanced across a second-hand copy of *Decision and Control* for £1.50 (one of
the perks of being a bookseller). It seemed rather technical and tough going to
me and it remained on my bookshelves unread for a long time. It was early 1979
that I came across *Platform for Change*; it had curiously coloured pages and at
least there were large sections that were not too difficult to comprehend.
Nevertheless, it certainly stretched me: I had never come across a book like this
before. It introduced important notions new to me, including 'metalanguage',
'metasystem' and 'recursion'. At the same time, I was also reading *Steps to an
Ecology of Mind* by Gregory Bateson ('cybernetics is the biggest bite out of the
Tree of Knowledge that mankind has taken in the last 2000 years') and *Tools for
Thought* by C.H. Waddington, the latter a good graphic guide for the layman of
the new topological terrain of systems thinking. These books completely
changed my perspective on the world as they enhanced my conceptual outlook
and I found myself in a holistic universe of dynamic interconnections and
relationships. Meanwhile, Eno continued to cite *Brain*; it was also mentioned in
another interview that he had just finished a chapter for a book edited by Beer.

It was sometime in late 1980 that, out of frustration at not finding the book, I wrote to Stafford Beer care of his publisher John Wiley. I heard nothing for some months until one day in March 1981 a large envelope dropped through my letter box. It contained the first of many letters from Stafford.

Cwarel Isaf 22nd March 1981

Hello David

Sorry for delay: I was in USA, & then comes the backlog!

I'm glad that you are 'seeing connections', & offer you this paper – which is hard going, but you seem to have the background.

Since *Platform*, Wiley has published my *The Heart of Enterprise* (1979) & *Brain of the Firm*, 2nd edn (1981). With any luck they are not yet remaindered in your shop!

The block with maths is very common. I advise you to distinguish between Spencer Brown & the others (who are using the full power of historical maths) – since he invents his own from scratch. I feel that you could master it – *Laws of Form*, that is. Just work at it, a few pages at a time: you could be amazed! It's very Taoistic. Do you know Jung's *Septem Sermones ad Mortuos*? Could be a bridge for you. If you do want to have a fresh go at classical math, the book is *Calculus Made Easy* by Sylvanus Thompson, which has been on the go for 70 years! It takes as its motto: what one fool can do another can.

I know/knew all but two of the people you mention: think of it as some kind of link. Eno too – though the book is held up. I have too much on.

You'll notice that I don't recommend any formal courses. I think they would drive you crazy. I have some freedom in teaching at Manchester, because it is all post-graduate, but obviously there are admission barriers to that. (How I disrespect the system...)

Tell me how you go

Peace

Stafford

I was immediately struck by the elegant calligraphic handwriting. The paper enclosed was *I Said, You Are Gods* – a lecture he had given to the Teilhard de Chardin Centre (to this day I still think this is one of the best things he ever wrote). The authors I had mentioned were: Arthur Koestler, Buckminster Fuller, George Spencer-Brown, Ludwig von Bertalanffy, Norbert Wiener, Bateson and Waddington. As regards *Laws of Form*, I discovered years later that Stafford had helped to fund Spencer-Brown during its writing; he had also given it an enthusiastic review for the journal *Nature* (Vol. 223 – Sept 1969), where he said 'I suspect I am reviewing a work of genius'. But it was the generosity of spirit and willingness to share (with a complete stranger) that most touched me in this first letter.

I had read the little volume of Jung many years before. Oddly enough it was also cited with much approval by Bateson.

Alas, the 'allergy' to maths persists!

Around this period I was reading a lot of William Blake and wrote to ask if he knew much of his work.

Cwarel Isaf Christmas Eve 1982

Happy Christmas David –

and thanks for your superb Zen picture. I was in Canada when you wrote it, in transit between Mexico and Venezuela. Too much travel, but here now for a month's respite.

You remind me of Blake. I have communicated with him solely through his art – & would like to try his prose. Moreover, I want to get hold of two books (referenced by Alan Watts): S. B. Dasgupta *An Intro to Tantric Buddhism* (Calcutta 1952) and Sir John Woodroffe *Shakti and Shakta* (Madras & London 1929).

It suddenly occurred to me that I know a second-hand bookseller! There are these commissions: can you accept them? (Even if you specialize in Systems Theory, these are right on the beam.)

The enclosed relates to a second – expanded – edition of poetry – notoriously difficult to market. The publishers plan a mail-order approach. Any ideas? It should be ready soon: not quite first-hand, you appreciate!

Shantih,

Stafford

Enclosed was a flier for his *Transit* with these reviewer comments: 'superbly realized' – 'skilful and graceful' – 'finely conceived and executed' – 'admire the tone, the diction, and control of mood and attitude' and I was curious to know who made these statements.

His interest in Indian metaphysics surprised and interested me as I had done some reading in this area, though I felt closer to Chinese Taoism and Japanese Zen, and still do.

In the meantime I sent Stafford a facsimile edition of Blake's *Urizen*.

15 Feb '83

Dear David,

I'm in the train on the way to USA and Mexico & trying to sew up some untied ends! Sorry for the delay – there was so much to do.

Most grateful for *Urizen*. I had read it, but never had a copy – it's fantastic. I understand that the art & the writing are a unity, especially here; but are there not prose works as such? Bateson appears to be quoting such.

Sorry about *Paradigm*: I think it has probably missed it's time. I'm engulfed & others have let me down. Eno is incommunicado again!

Advice on poetry – thanks. Something else that's not yet materialized – was due out in December. It has twice as many poems as the original *Transit*. The names of the critics were not given because permission had not then been sought. I'm not sure that anyone in UK has heard of Fred Cogswell, Order of Canada!

Glad you know *Septem Sermones* – most important...

I hope to get a major activity going in Mexico on this trip, so wish me luck. Hope this is legible – train bucking.

My best

Stafford

Challenge to Paradigm was the book of essays Stafford was editing and it's to our loss that it never did appear. Eno was not one of the contributors who let Stafford down; his piece *Self-Regulation and Autopoiesis in Contemporary Music* was completed, but never published (in fact it has since been lost – Appendix 4).

I soon managed to find one of the Tantric books in the Charing Cross Road.

Cwarel Isaf 5th April 1983

Dear David

Back – for only a month: I'm up to my eyes in Mexico now.

Many thanks for Blake-qua-gift: yes, please get *The Marriage* if you can.

It's expensive, but I'd like to acquire the Shakti book please: it's right at the centre of my yogic work.

The new edition of *Transit* has just come out in Montreal. The publisher, David Mitchell, is in London & I'm taking the liberty of giving him your name. You showed some interest, so I hope that you won't mind. At least you should get a copy! I'm interested in your reactions.

Best Wishes

Stafford

(The reference is to Blake's *The Marriage of Heaven and Hell*.)

Cwarel Isaf 21st April 1983

Dear David

So many thanks – cheque herewith.

I got straight into the book when the post came, abandoned my plans for the day, & stayed with it until 4am.

Yes: the Sanskrit is hard going (no glossary!), though I'm familiar with the background. Even more treacley is the post-Edwardian attitude to the Tantric sex...Despite this, I have understood the Panchatattva better than before. As you know, I teach this stuff to a small number of pupils. Sengupta next please.

Blake: great.

I don't know what/if to write. Capra didn't quite come off for me. Like Christmas Humphries: intellectually it's all there, but...give me rather Alan Watts. Have you read Capra's *Turning Point*? I'm halfway through. I'll probably meet him later this year – we're both due to speak at the American Soc. for Cybernetics.

Good luck with *Heart* & *Brain* & *Transit*.

I leave for Mexico on 1st May. Will be back (in Manchester) to teach first week of June – then here.

All kind thoughts

Stafford

Following Stafford's suggestion, I now read Alan Watts' autobiography *In My Own Way*; I also wrote to say I was pleased to see the Taoist philosopher Chuang-tzu (ca. 300 B.C.) in the bibliography of *Heart*.

Cwarel Isaf 14th January 1984

Dear David

I spent most of 1983 in Mexico (to which I lugged 'our' book) – hence no reply to your August letter.

Fancy Dover bringing out *Shakti* – I can't persuade anyone to read it because of the Sanskrit! I can explain about Arthur Avalon (a tiresome pseudonym): I am favouring Cerveza Oscura for myself (do you know Spanish?). He was Sir John Woodroffe, distinguished Indian civil servant; so he couldn't come clean until he retired. He's a thundering bore, but I've learned so much from his erudition.

I deserve a sweet for switching you on to Watts. Yes, his other books are great (try *The Joyous Cosmology* for the non-Beat version of Beat; but outstandingly *The Book*). However, can you sell me the autobiography which I haven't read!? Did he die of the booze? He was no spring chicken.

You remind me of the King Tut curse, whereby Lord Caernarvon & his pals were all struck down at the age of about 93!

Chuang-tzu: good, my ultimate favourite. Whitman, yes too. Again I'd like to buy him – I have nothing in the library.

Have you read Joan Jarra's *Victor* (Cape 1983)? It would give you all about 'my' Chile under Allende & I knew most of the people mentioned.

Here is one of the last 3 copies of *Transit*. I'll be grateful for your reactions. I have a quiet confidence in the stuff itself, especially read (tapes are available). I gave a reading in California in the fall that brought the house down.

Here's another fun question: I have been told (twice) about a Polish book called *Tadeusz Breza*. This apparently means 'The Door of Bronze'. So the question is whether some version of this is available in English – under any title! Author unknown!!

I can't go on with all this! We must meet sometime...

Love & peace

Stafford

The word 'tantra' comes from the Sanskrit root tan meaning 'to extend, to expand'. It is a highly ritualistic philosophy of psycho-physical exercises, with a strong emphasis on visualization, including concentration on the yogic art of mandalas and yantras. The aim is a transmutation and expansion of consciousness where the 'boundary' or sense of separation of the self from the universe at large dissolves. For Stafford this went hand in hand with cybernetic and systems methodology and epistemology.

Cwarel Isaf 23rd Feb. 1984

Dear David

Many thanks for the letter and books. Here's for Whitman: to make a present of Watts is most kind. I have read it before writing this. What a ghastly account Watts gives of his Big Sur life – such a degree of self-love & self-indulgence...

(Not that I mind a bit of fun! I was dancing in uninhibited fashion around the open fire at the Nepenthe restaurant (where he was with Kim Novak) only last October...)

Still – fascinating. He is a great gift to the neophyte.

Naturally I'm chuffed that you like *Transit*. I have got the tapes & people in Canada say they're helpful. I have done readings in Canada & USA. But there's no point in doing them here until copies arrive.

All good wishes

Stafford

Cwarel Isaf 30th May '84

Dear David

Was in the USA in April & bought *The Way of the Shaman* in the Yes! bookshop in Washington (a favourite place). Not so good as expected.

Returned via Vienna; opened the Euro-Cyb Conf. there; a dead city, manipulating its ghosts.

As you know I'm 'up to here' in Indian philosophy. I'd like *Physics as Metaphor* and also the *Hallucinogens* book on your rec. please.

Anyway, I continue to write poetry as well as phil., science, mgt... oh dear. There is overload.

I'm going to the USA on 18 June – a strange meeting in Minnesota planned by Bateson while still with us & then onto Canada for July.

I'm expecting to be 'Aritist (woops) in Residence' at the McLuhan Institute in the fall, there in Toronto.

I'll be here during August.

All this so's you know I've not deserted if I'm silent!

Please use your initiative on my behalf – you know how my mind operates...but better not send books here unless you know I'm here to receive them.

My best

Stafford

Cwarel Isaf 6th September '84

Dear David

Hope you're still there to receive these (intended goodies). I'm just leaving again – Paris, to collect the Wiener Gold Medal (oh!), then Canada.

Here's the promised book. Don't like it – massively self-indulgent. Or maybe I'm reacting to my mentor's dying in front of my eyes. But see final para: good. Sure thing, Warren.

Our Bateson meeting was fantastic. I just hope that they do something sensible with 17 90-minute audio tapes...

Here are more needs: Thich Nhat Hanh *The Miracle of Mindfulness*; *Report to Greco* & *The Stone Monkey* – no provenance, I heard they're famous. Can you help?

I think it was you who gave me *Physics as Metaphor* – was it? If so, mighty thanks. It's better than *The Tao of Physics* I think.

I've been under much pressure & have a lot of pain – excuse haste. The tapes with my love. Do say what you think!

My best

Stafford

The 'goodies' were two cassettes of Stafford reading his poetry, it was great to hear his handsome voice for the first time, and a book by Mary Catherine Bateson (daughter to Gregory Bateson and Margaret Mead) *Our Own Metaphor: A Personal Account of a Conference on the Effects of Conscious Purpose on Human Adaptation* held in 1968 in Austria. Participants included Bateson, Warren McCulloch and Gordon Pask.

Cwarel Isaf 12th January '85

Dear David

A quick Xmas visit – returning to Canada in a couple of weeks.

Glad you liked the poems. Tiresome of you to complain about some without saying which! Are they merely those used to illustrate my approach to scansion – as the notes explain? Otherwise, there are a couple I wouldn't have included, which others wanted in – but they are in no sense mathematical

I got *Stone Monkey* (about ancient Chinese science – very good, though badly paranoid) and *Report to Greco*: I can't understand its reputation.

Why do you ask about Eno? Anyway – to my total surprise he turned up in Toronto & attended a bunch of my seminars. It was great. I've got all his music. He gave me the latest, called *The Pearl*.

I have had trouble with pain – am getting it fairly organized I think. Hate taking pills.

In some haste.

My best

Stafford

Cwarel Isaf 3rd April 1985

Dear David

Got your card in Toronto & letter here. Many thanks.

The McLuhan job was for the fall term alone.

What did my seminars cover? Everything! I called them Applied Epistemology.

I couldn't manage the book that included Eno. Sad. Glad you reminded me – must do something about that.

Transit – oh well, cynghaneddion are by definition 'contrived'. Not really an experiment. Supposed to be impossible in English – as is the Sanskrit metre of *Tigers at Play*. Do you mean Anatol Rapoport? If so, I'll ask him about it. He lives round the (Toronto) corner.

Thrilled about the books. Do you think that you can get them here by

Saturday 13th? If so, hurry! If not, please hold until I return – but that will be June or July. I'm flying on 16th following the launch of my new book on Monday 15th at the Athenaeum Club, Pall Mall, 11am.

If you can possibly come please do & we can meet at last! I can't take delivery of books there, because of the travelling, except for *The Miracle* which I much want to read. Oh hell – if they are not too bulky, why don't we try it? I do have my tantric pupils in Canada...

Hey, this is a good idea. Can do? You must come to town sometimes!

What was holding me back is that I'll have to lug a number of my own new book back over the Atlantic. Oh well.

Respond, my friend!

Love & peace

Stafford

Cynghannedd means 'harmony' in Welsh. It is an exceptionally intricate system of sound-patterning involving assonance, alliteration and internal rhyme.

The books in question were a collection of studies on Tibetan Tantrism plus James Lovelock's *Gaia*. The new book from Stafford was *Diagnosing the System*. I can't recall what the Rapoport query was about (he was the man who developed the idea of non-zero-sum games).

Cwarel Isaf 10th April '85

Wednesday night

Thanks for card confirming Monday. HOWSOMEVER: Book launch is cancelled owing to lack of interest. Violent change of plan, therefore, as I don't have to travel on Sunday. PLEASE still come. I should like to entertain you to drinks at the Club between 6.0 & 8.0. Hope that's convenient. I still want the books too! So sorry can't go on to dinner – clients flying in from Europe.

Look forward to 6.0 & will show you over the joint. Yes – even I wear a tie (sometimes!).

My best

S.

I had only ever walked past the Athenaeum and saw it as a somewhat forbidding establishment. I was therefore nervous on arrival (I had forgotten the damn tie and had hastily purchased one around the corner). Stafford gave me a warm welcome and quickly made me feel at ease, particularly when he handed me a glass of choice wine. The place was the epitome of comfort, we sat by the fire and Stafford presented me with a copy of the new book 'hot from the press'. The man was always brimming largesse. He had a strong presence and looked distinguished, in an informal way, with his tweed jacket, handsome beard and gleeful eyes. He did indeed show me around and we walked up the great marble staircase to the library. He pointed out, with some pride, the list of Nobel prizewinners who had been members – more than any other club. He said that he was now part of a pressure group to allow women to join. When his other guests arrived I took my leave feeling quite exhilarated (he always had that effect on me). I left him with some books by the hilarious and profound Irish writer Flann O'Brien (*At Swim Two Birds*, *The Third Policeman*, *The Dalkey Archive*, *The Poor Mouth*).

We had talked about Zen and my favourite writer on the subject was, and still is, R. H. Blyth (who had lived in Japan during and after the war), Stafford didn't have any of his books – so that was soon rectified.

Cwarel Isaf 5th September '85

Hello David

Many thanks. If you persist in giving books away, you'll go bust! The Zen looks great, though I had heard that Blyth is idiosyncratic.

I'm really enjoying *Swim* & may even prefer it to *Policeman III*. I enjoyed both the Flanns you gave me in London, but not so much. Why do I feel so uneasy about his treatment of Joyce in *Dalkey* – even though, or perhaps because, they were personal friends...

I should love the Bharati if you can spare it. I so agree with you about the ugliness of much that is presented as the erotic tradition & have often wondered whether those prints were not the then-equivalent of dirty postcards! Hence all my searching (Shakti etc) for the truth of the matter, which is most beautiful. But that is essentially Indian, not Chin/Jap. By far the best modern book is *The Tantric Way* – know it? Can't recall author/pub: it's in Canada...

As is my Shakti, or will be in a few days, deo gratias.

I don't need Watlawick – quite close enough to that whole gang. But as usual I take your rec. as to Wilber.

Here's the Ludwig von B: good luck.

There's no hardback of *Transit*. My new ruse is to send copies of it to the 2 major poetry mags. Should they go bananas over it, I could perhaps interest the BBC in the tapes. But of course I'm not in the poetry establishment – 'haven't paid my dues'...

The new book is *Pebbles to Computers: the Thread* Oxford, June 1986. Don't worry – you'll get it!

Two anthologies of my voluminous past writings are planned. Other priorities, I fear.

Painting now. Wait til I tell you (Flann (c)). I've managed to collect no less than 30 fairly representative pictures & have just got slides & photos – bloody expensive! Let's see what the SB foundation make of that.

Must go – still have VAT to do.

Love

Stafford

The Bharati book was *The Tantric Tradition*; the Watlawick was *The Invented Reality*; the Wilber was *Up From Eden: the Evolution of Consciousness*; he had also sent me his Ludwig von Bertalanffy lecture *Death is Equifinal* which he had written simultaneously with his Teilhard lecture.

In the meantime I had 'bumped' into Stafford with some of his family at the National Theatre (where I had a bookstall) and we had a good chat at the bar there. I had recently informed him that my wife, Penny, and I were expecting a visit from the stork down the big chimney.

Cwarel Isaf 9th January 1986

What-ho David –

& congrats on the baby! Great.

Pictures: I must have made a joke about Flann which you didn't get. What was it? Mystery to me. Sorry to sound so peremptory.

Could we meet in the Athenaeum on Thursday 23rd? The slot (drinks available!) is 11-12.30. Sorry lunch is foreclosed (new pres of the OR Socy). It's the only chance. Let me know, please: if it's on, & I'll show you my pics. Otherwise –

I thought I was well founded in Zen; but the *Mumonkan* is pure joy. Well done David. What about the others in the series?

Love

Stafford

The series were Blyth's *Zen & Zen Classics* in 5 volumes.

At the club again, and Stafford showed me some photos of his paintings. They made me think of early Mondrian and Paul Klee. In addition he showed me the manuscript for *Pebbles*, he had designed the layout very carefully with a red pen acting as a graphic thread meandering from page to page. (When the book came out he was shocked to see that the publisher had reduced its dimensions, leaving the 'thread' to disappear off some pages; and perhaps insult was added to injury when a reviewer said it looked as if some child had been let loose with a red crayon!)

In May I sent him an account of the excitement of becoming a parent.

Cwarel Isaf 15th September '86

Hi David –

and many congrats to Penny & you on Alice. Yes, I know the feeling & never got blasé after 8 goes!!

I was waiting for the book to come before writing – but it never arrived! Hope it's there when I get to Toronto in a few days time. Yes, I'm leaving – it's been abominably hectic a visit, sorry not to have seen you.

One reason is that I have another 'Chile' – at last. Confid'ly it's for the new civilian President of Uruguay. Very exciting, but I've had a great many things to do since I got over here.

All this has slowed my reading. However I studied Blyth with care: marvellous. It seems he didn't complete his project with the other texts...

Beards I have just finished this trip. Read it in bed in this cottage. Tremendous! Many thanks. Hell's teeth: how little one knows!!

Forgive haste

Love

Stafford

(I had sent Stafford a serious book on the history of beards, which is known as pogonotrophy, from the Greek pŏgŏn meaning 'beard' – honest!)

Cwarel Isaf Epiphany '87

Dear Man:

Thrilled about Dasgupta. I'm leaving Saturday (things have been hell – massive overload) & want to take it to Canada. I am overnight at club on 15th. In Manchester before then. Can we meet somehow, I ask. You could leave things for me perhaps... Write more! What else is there?

Could speak on phone from Business School, or see you there! Any Manchester trade? How are you fixed?

Meanwhile am sending on an unopened copy of *Pebbles* with my love. Whoopee for Alice! I know all about it. You may survive.

Stafford

I did meet Stafford at the club quite early, about 9am, (date uncertain). He was startlingly under the weather and was on anti-biotics from a bad fall. We had a clumsy encounter there, as I had the usual carrier bag of books. I accompanied him, via taxi, to Heathrow and helped him through the check in. (We had a good conversation in the taxi about Borges' remarkable fictions.) I watched him walk, with a heavy gait, down the long corridor; he never once looked back...

Toronto 15th November 1987

Hello David

Thanks for writing – & taking so much trouble.

What I'm really saying, I suppose, is would you like to be the UK agent for this book & if so how would that work? For example, you could insert a flier in the journals whose readership knows me, & supply by mail order (you must be used to posting books). Since the technology is fun, the art mags might work too. All these things... I'm hoping to have a mock-up when I hit London for Xmas.

In particular I'm lecturing at City Univ. on 14th Jan & may come up a day or so earlier. Let's try to meet? The idea would be to evolve a deal & put it to a publisher. Incubate!

I'll get someone to look for Roszak – never heard of him.

Good luck with Jim Miller!! (an old friend). I think that the cognoscenti have not at all forgotten Korzybski. Wilden I don't know. Marv Minsky is another old friend: I disagree with him about almost everything! And I've often denounced the term AI.

Hey, I 'lost' a book in the war which I couldn't replace because I forgot both title & author. He said: 'If shit had a high market value, the poor would be born without arseholes.' I've just seen a reference to *Religion & the Rise of Capitalism*, R. H. Tawney, 1936. THAT'S IT. I recognize it now. Can you find it for me? Tawney was a prof at LSE I think, alongside Harold Laski. Heigh ho, hold it if you find it.

Here's something you should be interested in: *The Lion Path: You Can Take It With You* by Musaios. I think the author is C. A. Muses, a distinguished mathematician. It's all Egyptology & numerology. Ingenious. Any report?

Love & peace

Stafford

I can't remember what ever came of the art project.

I had pointed out to Stafford that Theodore Roszak had been critical, in an ill informed way, of the work that was done in Chile.

I had just acquired a copy of *Living Systems* by Jim Miller; a massive tome (it made *War and Peace* look like a quick read!) which weighed down my shelves for a few years, untouched, before I sold it to pay the gas bill.

Korzybsky was the founder of General Semantics whose famous maxim was: 'the map is not the territory'.

Marvin Minsky was a leading proponent of Artificial Intelligence. Stafford told me that they had spent time cooped up together on some exotic island at a conference hosted by Arthur C. Clarke. The problem with AI, as far as Stafford was concerned, was that no one had yet given him a satisfactory definition of what 'intelligence' actually is.

I quickly found the Tawney book.

In January '88 Stafford phoned inviting me to the club again. This time he was on good form. The previous night he had given a talk *The Impact of Systems Thinking on Government* to The Institute of Measurement & Control; I had gone along hoping to hear it – but to the wrong venue!

In April I produced my first catalogue of books, all on the history of ideas, with a strong slant towards cybernetics and systems theory.

The Athenaeum 7th May '88

Hi David –

You are (so far!) infallible. Here's my cheque.

I'll send *Metagame* to you for contemplation. More later, on this & the paintings.

We must meet in Aug/Sept, & I'll take responsibilty to initiate that.

Renewed congrats on the catalogue. Need to peruse it. MBS lists? I guess that falls for me to chase....

Love

Stafford

Toronto July 14th '88

Hello David

I'm going quietly mad: this is the letter I thought I wrote in May... Fact is, I've found your last letter, neatly stored with these enclosures, in the wrong pile. Sorry.

Oh yes, do collect the lost masterpieces. We recently picked up 2 copies of Spencer Brown & a *Human Use of HB* ($1). I wish to God someone would republish *Heart*.

YES: you can get a World Passport. That's why I gave the address. Write to Garry Davis himself in NYC (he's currently running for President of the USA, bless him) & mention me. Costs of course (?$25).

Thanks so much for the Leibnitz piece: it explains so much about the

Monadology to know this. I'm sorry to say that I bounced off Needham's massive ego. Hope you like this preface.

Here at last is *Metagame* (no news at all of the paintings book). This cost about a dollar to produce. So what do you say? The foundation would like to make some money on it if poss! How much is it worth & what is the bookseller's cut? I'm coming to UK in August to end September & of course we must meet. But should I bring copies of *Metagame* & if so how many? I'm going to Venezuela on Saturday for two weeks.

Book yourself at home with BBC 2 on 14 Sept. (That should have you guessing!) Must go.

Love & peace

Stafford

The cv is to help you consider strategies, mailings, flyers? Why not ask the OR Society the cost of an insert or an announcement in the Newsletter?

In a previous conversation Stafford was surprised to hear that the German philosopher Leibnitz (1646-1716) had been influenced by the ancient Chinese oracle the *I Ching*. He had studied a partial Jesuit translation and the notions of yin and yang influenced his development of binary mathematics. I sent Stafford an article about this by the great Sinologist Joseph Needham (who Stafford appears to have met!). Soon afterwards Stafford sent me a preface to the book *The Identity of Organizations* by Elkin & Schvarstein into which he incorporated some of this information.

I became the UK distributor for Stafford's epic poem *One Person Metagame* and his daughter, Vanilla, designed the flyer.

The BBC repeated a documentary they had shown from the early 1960s that included Stafford and Kingsley Amis talking about the future of society followed by a studio discussion between the two men 25 years on. In *The Guardian* the following day a TV critic referred to Professor Beer as having a beard like a towel roll!

I now had another new catalogue out.

Toronto October 26 1988

Hello David;

Many thanks for the books. It was clever of you to spot Muses – and as you know Blyth is always welcome. I also have to thank you for your little birthday present, which is much appreciated. I have read the whole thing, and (as you will expect) I know many of the anecdotes. But there were many that I did not know and I have thoroughly enjoyed the whole thing. I must also thank you for trying to promote *Metagame*: Vanilla tells me that there has so far been no takers, but that's life.

On the question of the Spurious: I am tempted to put my money on #178. Seminal work indeed. But I know that you are prone to pretty little jokes, so probably that is not the clue. If the book really exists, I think I would like to buy it...but the price is a bit steep!

Now may I ask you a little favour? Number 340, which I do not want to buy, concerns a meeting whose silver jubilee is to be celebrated next year at Queen's College Cambridge – and I have to give the keynote speech. Well, I am totally aware that I was there, and I remember giving tongue – certainly as Chairman of a session. But I am not sure whether I made a major address or not. Would it be too much trouble for you to check out what the record is as far as my participation was concerned? I can tell you that my intention at this moment is to hit them so hard next April that I will make the Sunday papers.

Love & peace

Stafford

The present was a little book called *Vicious Circles & Infinity: an Anthology of Paradoxes* by Hughes & Brecht.

My catalogues always contained an imaginary book and there was a prize for the first person to spot it. #178 was *Phallic Worship* (which I said was a seminal study!) and it did indeed exist.

The silver jubilee was for the Operational Research Society, I can't remember what the book in question was.

Toronto 9th March 1989

Hi David!

I'm supposed to be in Venezuela, but guess wot...

Thanks so much for the tape: your tastes are clear! You are right about the Cosmic Master. Can you believe that there finds itself a dive in Caracas called the Johann Sebastian Bar?

Here are two of the three things you asked me for. I've reread my old mentor: he's amazing. The Varela/HHDL article got pitched I'm afraid (as well it might).

Thanks for catalogue 3. If you still have them, please keep 123, 427, 430 for me. I'll be in Europe all April. Raúl & I are spending some of 4th/5th in the Club. Sir John Eccles is speaking at Kings & I've never met him – Brit. Cyb. Soc. Interested? If not, would it be convenient to look into the

Club 9.30 on 5th? Raúl can spare me for half an hour I guess! I have to go to the Eccles reception on 4th afterwards, but will try to get there early.

Told Russ (unattrib!) what you said, He replies: 'Recall my earlier statement which still stands – I have learned more from my disagreements with you than from my agreements with most people.' The poor man & his brand new wife have been badly hurt by a drunken driver.

I'm giving the banquet address at Queen's Cambs on 16th April for the ORS. Russ expects to come...

I have finished 9 of the 10 *Requiem* paintings. There is talk of hanging them in the chancel of Christchurch here – a good start, if so.

Love

Stafford

At this time I was going through a Bach phase and sent Stafford a tape of favourite pieces.

His old mentor was Warren McCulloch: neurocybernetician, blacksmith and poet.

HHDL was His Holiness the Dalai Lama, for whom Stafford had profound respect. I remember him disapproving of an encounter where Francisco Varela harangued HHDL about the human brain and consciousness.

Russ is Russell Ackoff, an old sparring partner.

I subsequently received Stafford's Banquet Address '*I am the Emperor – and I Want Dumplings*'.

Toronto 15th May 1989

Hello David

Many thanks for the books – I like to get your cheque off at once, for heaven knows I can't imagine how you make enough to live on!

But I hope you'll respond to my latest writings in due course.

I'm leery of Leary!!!

Love

Stafford

I had told Stafford that the guru of psychedelics, Timothy Leary, referred to himself as a cyber-shaman! This was in reference to a chat we had about the sad abuse and misapplication of the word 'cybernetics'. He agreed we now needed a new word (this prompted a story about when he was going through customs somewhere, and the customs officer asked what he was a professor of: 'Cybernetics' said Stafford, 'I know what that is' replied our official with pride 'it's when you freeze dead bodies to be brought back to life at some future date...').

The latest writings were quite a surprise: *The Chronicles of Wizard Prang*. The term came from the wartime RAF pilots who referred to a crash as a 'wizard prang'. The chronicles are in the form of playful, philosophical parables with an old wizard (bearing more than a passing resemblance to the author, whose favoured tipple was also wine and water) living in a remote cottage. The humour is self-deprecating – many of his spells backfire. It has been described as a kind of fairy tale for grown ups. Its style certainly allowed Stafford great freedom to explore wide ranging metaphysical issues about the nature of being and becoming, sex and the illusions of time (or in short 'life, the universe and everything'). This note graced the cover:

This copy goes to a friend who expressed interest, his/her spouse and older children (Parental Guidance!). I am longing to know what you make of it, and whether I have omitted any major topic on which the wizard would have observations. (Illustrations in the style of Ronald Searle or Gerald Scarfe. No chi-chi little wizards in conical hats.)
Love and peace – **Stafford**

I happened to have a Ronald Searle book in stock and there was a perfect cartoon of a wizard which I photocopied and embellished appropriately (with apologies to Mr Searle!) and sent to an appreciative Stafford. More solemnly, my father had recently died and in grief I asked the wizard about confronting the great mystery of death. A few months later another package arrived with more Prang material and this note:

David – Ch 17 becomes 20. 3 new chapters. This is for you...it is pretty difficult I fear. Love **S.**

Chapter 17 was indeed difficult, but I was deeply moved that so much thought and feeling had gone into responding to my plea.

As a small token of thanks I sent him a copy of *Tristram Shandy* by Laurence Sterne; first published in 1760, it remains one of the most inventive, playful and unusual books ever written. Stafford really enthused about it.

The next letter, a personalised circular, was the start of something completely new that would absorb Stafford for the rest of his days. This is a much edited version.

Manchester Business School 5th December 1989

Dear David

This is an invitation to an Extraordinary Meeting that I hope to hold at the Manchester Business School over the 'long' weekend January 26th (starting 6.00 pm) and breaking up after lunch in the 29th. A room will be provided for you for the three nights Friday, Saturday, Sunday because the meeting will not be a respecter of ordinary hours. People may wish to go on late. Then we shall also provide the usual three meals a day (plus morning and afternoon breaks).

You may remember the 'agendaless' meetings that I have held for twenty years – meetings which evolve their own agenda. Disliking the negative term, I now call such a meeting The Problem Jostle. A brand new social invention I call Team Syntegrity (after Bucky Fuller's 'tensile integrity'). This is a protocol whereby thirty people are called upon to use the Problem Jostle technique in order to identify twelve issues that they would like to discuss. Perhaps you have immediately spotted that the model is an icosahedron and that the protocol is geodesic...

The two techniques in tandem are supposed to define a perfect democracy. There is no scope for the emergence of hierarchy. The world seems to be in dire need of such an organisational approach.

The scenario I propose for the January meeting is precisely that of (wait for it!) the future of the world... You will find enclosed a paper entitled 'Easier Done Than Said'. It is addressed to 'about Twenty Friends' around the world whom I hope to cajole into running a meeting such as the January meeting in Manchester.

I am inviting you personally – rather than throwing this open to the world citizenry – because we need exactly thirty people and because this is a pioneer occasion. That means in turn that, if you do not already know the invited participants, you will find them intellectually congenial. Hooray for synergy.

Finally then, I plead for your help. First of all, COME! However... I have not taken leave of my statistical senses. This loose procedure is not going to result in the arrival of exactly thirty people – unless we invoke feedback.

Love and peace

Stafford Beer

Of course I couldn't resist this appeal. It was an amazing weekend. I'm not much of a joiner but it was a pleasure meeting so many of Stafford's colleagues including his partner from Toronto, Allenna Leonard. There proved to be a few teething problems with the mathematical structure of the event that took some ironing out. I for one came away feeling hopeful that we had indeed pioneered a potent new model for conflict resolution.

(Once, at the Club, Stafford told me that Buckminster Fuller had sat on the very chair I was on and he was so small that his feet didn't touch the floor!)

Toronto 3rd May 1990

Dear David

Thanks so much for the Pärt music: quite extraordinary. Vanilla has been on about him for some time – did you turn her on to it?

Glad you enjoyed Manchester. I am just now trying to write it up ready for some work with Pacific Bell in San Francisco in 3 weeks time. & at St Gallen June/July. Of course you will get what I write. The business was marred by the very fact that so pleased you (& me): all these people are so nice that the usual tensions were missing!

I'm due in Wales 4-16 June & 23 July-4 Aug, Switzerland intervening. No details.

Was in Mexico & got a real nasty – hence delay in writing. Thanks for so much that I haven't thanked you for properly – Wiener/Eliot etc.

Must have told you that I'm getting a Chair at UC Swansea. The library is getting some books when they hear from me! I shall give your name as an optimal supplier of out-of-p. books (I'm assuming they are 'tied' for new vols). I'm writing a Primer for Undergrads for my nice new course. 'Alternative Talk About Managing' – sellable?

I simply haven't had time to bother with *Prang* or *Requiem*.

You seem to have dropped me from the Spring Catalogue: I thought we were winning?! I'm probably misunderstanding your system.

Must push on: not much of a literary effort – but touching base.

My best

Stafford

I had sent Stafford a tape of the Estonian composer Arvo Pärt.

I noticed, in a volume of T. S. Eliot's letters, that Eliot and Norbert Wiener had been at Cambridge University at the same time and there was an interesting account of a Christmas Day they spent together.

Next came an intriguing request.

Toronto 17th May 1990

Dear David,

I hope you got a fairly chatty letter from me, and I am persona grata as a result...

HELP! We have had desultory conversations in the past about my personal library, which is at Sallie's house in Llandysul. Does everyone share my difficulty in trying to guess the number of books? It's probably far less impressive than I have led you to think. Anyway, opportunity has quite suddenly opened up at the Institute for Science and Technology at the Liverpool Poly. They want 'a valuation of the library so that this can be factored into the business plan for the Foundation'. How to proceed?

I am due in Wales in three weeks time. I expect to hit the Athenaeum by noon on June 4th. I'm booked for a family lunch, but I'm wondering if you would find it at all convenient to be bought some drinks while we chew the fat over this for an hour? Don't make sacrifices; but a tête-a-tête would be much easier to handle the complications. I'll be leaving for Wales in the afternoon, so this is rather a small window.

Love & peace

Stafford

I met Stafford at the Club and he explained further that Liverpool John Moores University were planning to set up the Stafford Beer Collection. We were short on time, so I met him again that afternoon at Paddington Station; we travelled part of the journey together (I had to change at Swindon) and this gave us the chance to plan a visit to his library in detail: I would go to Llandysul the following week for a brief initial assessment and meet him in the evening in The Black Lion in Lampeter, I would then travel back to his cottage for the night. As a bibliophile I was really looking forward to this!

The collection didn't fail to impress. It was intriguing to find some of Stafford's very early writings including his own translations from ancient Greek and Sanskrit. There were manuscripts of many of his books, all hand written with real ink in a real fountain pen! (He once pointed out to me his trusty swivel barrelled pen; it had been given to him when he retired from the steel industry in the early '60s – alas, it was stolen in the '90s in Venezuela.) There too was his 3-dimensional model of the algedonode featured in *Brain* and his Stochastic Analogue Machine. And of course many hundreds of books on philosophy, poetry, religion and science. But this was all going to take at least a full day to do some kind of estimate.

We duly met that evening and had a meal (The Black Lion was *one* of Stafford's locals) before I followed his Land Rover into the hills of Ceredigion.

Arriving at the cottage felt almost like a rite of passage. I had written to this address so often – Cwarel Isaf, which means 'lowest lying quarry' – that the place had an almost sanctified aura for me. (It had been a school house attached to a slate quarry, with a railway running behind it; in fact a local man, Mr William Lewis, was hit by a train here and killed in September 1934.)

When he first moved here in the mid '70s there was a good deal of militant Welsh nationalist activity in the area and outsiders with 'weekend' homes experienced some hostility (a comic slogan of this period read: 'Come home to a real fire – buy a cottage in Wales!'). With this in mind Stafford had the good sense to have a sign on the walls saying: 'Meibion Glyndwr! Peidiwch a Llosgi fy Mwthyn, Rwy'n byw yma!! Athro Cwrw' meaning 'Sons of Glyndwr! Don't burn my cottage, I live here!! Professor Beer'. Cwrw, pronounced 'kooroo', is Welsh for beer.

It was a small compact bulding, down a steepish slope (it was clear why Stafford needed a four wheel drive vehicle!). Inside resembled a kind of Aladdin's cave. It was simple, frugal, almost cell like; nevertheless it contained many exotic, but unsophisticated, objects collected from around the world: a spinning wheel, flutes and drums (from Chile), tapestries, carvings (including one superb Indian erotic embrace). There was an open fire with a large foot bellows and piles of logs. Books, papers and journals in fairly neat stacks. On the walls were various slogans that had importance for Stafford, including 'THINK BEFORE YOU THINK' and 'TAT TVAM ASI' a transliteration from the Sanskrit meaning 'Thou Art That'. It was a highly personal place, like looking into Stafford's head; perhaps a good example of organised chaos? Incense also filled the air. The spinning wheel was a clue to an important role model for Stafford: Mahatma Gandhi. He had heard Gandhiji speak twice while serving in India.

Little did I realise we were in for the long haul. We sat and talked and drank wine deep into the night, in fact the sun was coming up when we retired. And I don't think that there was anything under that sun we hadn't discussed! The following morning he was wide awake early and still full of ideas – I certainly wasn't... He had been reading Chuang-tzu in bed and was very amused to find this comment: 'How can I tell whether the dead are not amazed that they ever clung to life?'.

I also thought how curious it was to be sitting in an austere Welsh quarry with Stafford and on another occasion to be sitting in the opulence of the Athenaeum!

A few weeks later I went to value the library. I was fine with the books but it wasn't easy putting a price on manuscripts, memorabilia etc.

Toronto 19th September '90

David:

The last four months have been hard going, and it has taken me too long to recover completely from a collapse while in Switzerland as guest professor last July. I'm pretty much OK now, but miles behindhand.

Thanks for evaluation: as you say, though, it leaves unanswered questions re MSS, paintings (!) memorabilia…ouch.

Only query about books you took is Mgt Sc. The books (except duplicate *Brain/Heart*) on the mantelpiece are all different editions – I kept an example of all that came my way. Pointless? You'd know. I'm not bothered.

Thanks for snaps. I'll bring 6 copies (all we have in stock) of *Designing Freedom* @ £5 a throw. OK? We can easily get more…

Requiem has been prof. phot'd – 8 x 11 – looks impressive. But there are 10 paintings, so a set will cost £40 (expressed as £4 each, sounds better!). Can you sell that?!

Perhaps the Club on 9th (eve) or 10th (lunch)? Please drop a note to Wales.

Love – **Stafford**

There had been duplicates of books in the collection which I had offered to purchase separately for my own reading (with respect to my unsupervised access to all of this, Stafford said 'I trust you as much as I trust my own brother'; I wasn't quite sure how to take that!). I was now a distributor for *Designing Freedom*.

Cwarel Isaf 2nd Oct '90

Hi David – I'm here.

OK for 10th. I'll show you big new photos of *Requiem*.

The box of tapes are *Metagame* (me, with Mark's musical interludes) & other poems from *Transit*. We have covers & I'll try to bring a set. Can it be that we haven't discussed this before?

I'll be at the club from 12.0 to 4.0 that day. Come early if poss. If you're late, we can still go to a pub.

Love

Stafford

I was treated to a slap up three course lunch with splendid wines. After this we retired to the library and sat in leather wing backed chairs quaffing and looking at some of the books. Stafford got down an enormous edition of *The Egyptian Book of the Dead* which he said he had almost finished reading after a couple of decades! We had a particularly memorable session. I was now distributor for his tapes.

Cwarel Isaf Halloween (!) '90

Hi David –

Tried to phone often during MBS week: I think you're away...

Remembered the 'something else' I mentioned at the Club. Books, indeed: TA-RA.

High time I caught up with this stuff & have strong recommendation: John Stevens *Sacred Calligraphy of the East* – Shambhala 1981. Know it?

Dipped into Sallie's library book, which heard of but dismissed: seems wrongly... Leo Abse, *Margaret Daughter of Beatrice* – likely to turn up 2nd hand? It caused a stir, but momentarily.

Reiterated thanks for your help at L'pool. It's all happening!

Off to Swansea, Canada (please God) Saturday.

Love

Stafford

Toronto 9th July 1991

My Dear David

Feel terrible about missing you on recent trip – was racing round Durham, Manchester, Liverpool & Swansea: now have chairs in each! Pretty absurd. Hope you are aware of my affairs via others – especially the proposed installation of my *Requiem* in Paddy's Wigwam. Wildly exciting. Would like to do the music myself, with cybernetic weighting per picture per sensed viewer – but can't see how (I mean time & opportunity – the rest of it is easy!). Meantime: WHERE'S ENO? Reach him for me if at all possible.

Here's answers to your old letter:

Yes: please hold *Sacred Calligraphy* & let's make sure we meet in Oct/Nov (next trip).

How many *Designing F* do you want? Can bring. Also *Metagame* I guess! How did Sheldrake go? I have an open mind.

De Bono. Known him for years. Intellectual pirate, but does good at some level s'pose Amazed to be told that on Desert Island Discs he nominated *Platform* as extra to Bible & Bill the Quill. Can this be? Did your sales go up?!

Can't rattle on. Am writing book on Team Syntegrity – where amazing mathematical developments happen...

Sugar completely haywire after too much stress on trip (such as missing dear friends!). Am also awaiting some kind of (?) operation on throat for some kind of (?) stricture...unseemly. Even so, we are supposed to be in Amherst Mass for ASC Conf next week.

Love & peace

Stafford

Paddy's Wigwam is (it should go without saying) the Catholic Metropolitan Cathedral of Christ the King, Liverpool.

I wrote to Eno saying that Stafford needed him URGENT – there are times when it would be easier to contact the Pope than Eno – I heard later that he did indeed respond with suggestions to Stafford but nothing came of this 'collaboration'.

Rupert Sheldrake was the biologist who came up with the notion of 'morphic resonance'. He purchased a lot of books from me and I got to meet him at his home; I mentioned to Stafford that he had two sons called Merlin and Cosmo.

Toronto 23rd August 1991

My Dear David

Many thanks for your letter & for the delightful little book on Leibniz.

Interesting to get accounts from both you & Nil about the same occasion! Different emphases. The trouble with Gordon, if I may adopt his own style, is that he knows the trouble with everyone else. In my own case, to take an objective instance, he tells everyone that I have had heart attacks, & am at constant risk, & he tries to give people nitroglycerine to slip to me unbeknownst. I have never had a heart attack, my cholesterol & blood pressure are normal & a recent routine ECG is just fine.

But I have had trouble with my throat. Couldn't swallow. Seems I acquired what's called a 'web' that closes up the oesophagus. They pushed out like unblocking a drain – with rods of increasing size. It was thoroughly unpleasant. I had intravenous anaesthetics that were supposed to mean I wouldn't notice the assault. That's a bit of a joke, eh? I'm sure you wouldn't expect that to have any effect on my consciousness. I did both the *Guardian* crosswords while supposedly 'sleeping it off'.

Very interested about Sheldrake. My Harry's second name is Cosmo – watch it!

Please don't bother Eno or Fripp for the nonce. I take delivery of a synthesizer on Sunday.

Here are the latest pieces plus the Casti collaboration.

Love & peace

Stafford

I had been to lunch with Stafford's daughter Vanilla (Nil) and Gordon and Elizabeth Pask. Gordon reminded me of an early Doctor Who, he certainly looked the part of the eccentric (deranged even!) professor. A good man; but it is only recently that I've started to come to grips with his ideas. Gordon gave a very amusing account of how Spencer-Brown had written *Laws of Form* in their bath, over a six month period, while staying in the Pask household. I suspect Stafford and Gordon, as an item of sorts, go back centuries.

(More recently I read *My Time in Space* by the writer and cartographer Tim Robinson. This contains a fascinating account of Spencer-Brown and the four-colour map theorem. Robinson was the man who drew the distinctive symbols and diagrams for *Laws of Form*.)

Regrettably, this was not to be the last we heard of Stafford's throat problems.

The Casti piece was *Investment Against Disaster in Large Organizations* plus some work in progress on the Syntegrity book.

Toronto 10th April 1992

Dear David

So glad we had a bit of a chat. The Wiley news is exciting, eh?

Thanks so much for the loan of HvF. It has been useful to review how he handles the eigenvalue stuff. Haven't read Varela yet obviously!

Glad *DF* goes well, & many thanks for the Bach & Basho: a good combination indeed.

Kybernetes is doing a 92 page special edn on me next year: I'm a bit taken aback by this. Alex Andrew is writing an intro 'profile'...

For the first time in my life I couldn't vote Labour: whatever happened to Socialism? So I voted Plaid Cymru – & for the f.t.i.m.l. my man won!

Love

Stafford

Stafford's publisher, John Wiley, were planning to reprint many of his books in a uniform paperback edition, with paintings by Vanilla on the covers.

I had been in correspondence, and had spoken on the phone, with Heinz von Foerster, who lived in California. Known as 'the Socrates of Cybernetic thought', he had called Stafford 'the British wunderkind of cybernetics in management' (he was also a professional magician). Here was another generous soul. He sent me a bunch of his papers, difficult in those days to locate if you weren't a member of academe, and a book length study of his work: *The Dream of Reality* by Lynn Segal (Heinz addressed me as 'the maverick bookseller' – a label I approve of). I had lent these to Stafford.

In November I had visited the cottage again, with new translations of Lao-tzu's *Tao Te Ching* and Chuang-tsu which Stafford couldn't wait to read. We went out to lunch in a place called Little Piglets; it was a very wet day, even by Welsh standards! We were the only people in the restaurant until a funeral party arrived and filled up the tables around us, adding to the general gloom.

Cwarel Isaf 5th August 1992

Dear David

Sorry we missed a meeting on our brief vac: we did not get far enough east, As it was, 400 miles in the clapped-out Land Rover was enough. Allenna went back to Canada last week. I went to the South Bank with her first (Haywood: Magritte) & thought of you. Bookstalls not up to much!

Glad you're into poetry. I know all you list & of course *White Goddess*. Try Cynghanedd (see notes in *Transit*) – ballades are peanuts! Chinese medicine Sure! See *The Stone Monkey*. Which Varela am I supposed to have read? Muses isn't the only one doing these linkages: what do you think I've been up to all these years?!

Ah well – you'll detect the hurry. Canada beckons. Back for Liverpool: you should get official invitation to private showing on 25th Sept but it may take a few weeks. Prior warning. Please come.

Love

Stafford

I had now started seriously studying and writing poetry and was tentatively sending Stafford some of my work.

Requiem received its preview on Stafford's 66th birthday. It was a momentous event and it meant so very much to him. Many old and new friends were there (Stafford never stopped making friends). After all the speculation, the accompanying music turned out to be Requiems by Mozart, Bruckner, Faure and Durufflet. The problem was that there were too many people around and I'm sorry that I never got the chance to engage silently with the work on my own terms.

A few weeks later I visited Cwarel Isaf again. This time I took Stafford out to lunch in Lampeter in return for a 'masterclass' in poetry. I recall him saying that these early attempts were in need of aerating! He confessed that, like me, he sometimes over indulged in polysyllables. We talked about Welsh verse (cynghanedd) and Dylan Thomas, though he said that he had also learned much about the patterning of consonants from Shakespeare's sonnets.

Toronto Epiphany 1992

My Dear David

Happy New Year! This is simply about *Designing Freedom*. We have just sent you 24 copies by surface mail. I know that you didn't ask for so many, but I want to try the experiment that follows.

Prices have risen with the latest printing, & books now attract the iniquitous General Sales Tax of 7%. The price in the shops is $9.58 The 24 copies therefore cost $229.92 – & I have also incurred $22.65 in postage & insurance. So the cost at Oxford becomes $10.52 each. At today's rate of exchange (2.1179) that's virtually a fiver & my investment of $252.57 comes to £119.25.

This, but no more, needs to come back to me – sooner or later – because I have already had my cut through royalty & a purchase discount. So actually it's quite up to you what you charge beyond the fiver.

My suggestion is this. You can correctly advertise that the book is not obtainable in the UK, & I'd have thought that no one would baulk at £8. If that were the price (with you clearing £3) then I should like to tell my students that they can get it from you at the reduced rate of £7. by marking their orders 'SBS' (for SB Student). You would get only £2 clear on those! The point is that I should like to learn about the elasticity of demand – & such data would make a start.

Don't let me tie you in any way. I'll accept whatever you say, so long as I get back the outlay some day.

Still grinding on with Syntegrity...More later.

Love & peace

Stafford

It's worth mentioning, at this point, that Stafford put an enormous amount of business my way. He recommended me to people all over the world and hardly a day went by without someone ordering or searching for a book. I had my work cut out meeting the demand for so many out-of-print cybernetic and systems books. Pre-internet, there was no other way but to put in a lot of time getting through a good deal of shoe leather and tyre rubber. The catalogues proved to be useful for bringing me into contact with unusual characters. One day George Spencer-Brown phoned to tick me off for listing a first edition of *Laws of Form* at only £15. He said that such a masterpiece was worth hundreds! He talked for about an hour and told me how he had advertised his sperm for any woman who might want to have a genius for a child. In California women were queueing up to be intimate with the author of such a famous book. Who'd ever have thought that a little book of calculus could prove to be such a vigorous aphrodisiac?!

Cwarel Isaf 13th January 1993

Dear David

Your poetry is telling. It's natural to use this potent medium for grieving; however, I look forward to the expression of joy...As to our mutual sesquepedalion problem: a quick dose of Ted Hughes?!

Herewith an amended *Torment* (with thumbscrews?) & Part II of *Dispute*. I've tried to make it clear & also a 'good read'.

Leaving for India tomorrow. Back (DV) in 2 weeks & awaiting your verdict.

Love & peace

Stafford

McGinn *The Problem of Consciousness* – Danah Zohar *The Quantum Self* – Have a feeling you gave me the second, but can't find it...? Can you get them? You'll see why!

The text was *World in Torment: A Time Whose Idea Must Come*, his Presidential address to the World Organization of Systems & Cybernetics at their conference in New Delhi.

Cwarel Isaf 30th January 1993

Personal Bulletin

The conference was quite successful: it was closed by the Indian President singing a devotional song by Tagore in Bengali – unaccompanied. What a change!

My stuff was v. well received & I was compelled to give extra seminars outside – notably at the Nat Inst of Sc, Tec & Dev. The triage model was generally acclaimed. The 'softly, softly' approach to the WG syntegration certainly worked. I have recruited 5 more Keys (3 India (Delhi, Hyperabad, Kharagpur), 1 Aus, 1 UK). Sadly, no US people presented. Official view "The State Dept has advised against travel, due to unrest". Unofficially, the reaction was splenetic. WOSC – wise, there are disastrous financial consequences with (?) 100 bookings cancelled. Wiener's biographer Masani was an exception – but he is Indian! Glad to have met him at last – long story to bore you with...Of course Garry Davis would not have been daunted, but no visa.

It was wonderful to be back at spiritual home (with French wine at Rs 300 (£7) a glass – enough to make a smuggler of anyone, eh?). In answer to questions about my denunciation of capitalism I threw off a suggestion that India found an Int. Inst. of Vedantic Mgt. seized on avidly – had to do seminar 'What do you mean?' & even more enthusiasm generated. Now committed to write-up. However this will do fine for Churchman's Festschrift (overdue). Top priority. Will forward soon...

I have major speech in Bristol on 10th (on cybernetics of safety in eng. design).

Allenna is running syntegration for Democratic Left (as far as we know!). We're hoping to get a couple of days holiday in here somehow.

Oh – UK represented by Mike Jackson & Pete Dudley. Had amiable chat between their trips to Agra (Taj) & Jaipur (cricket): suitably English. Japanese, Greeks, French all there, but mostly Asiatic.

I'm a bit hassled!

Stafford

Cwarel Isaf 24 July '93

Hello David

At last I embark on a week (the last here this trip) devoted to no-one but myself. It's to review the state of the new book.

Thanks for your letter: reverse should interest you & wonder if you'll hear from them.

The poems are coming along fine, aren't they? Have you been reading Ted Hughes? The Valentine is suitably salacious! Comes off.

I didn't remember Brough when I read your letter, but have clawed him back. Warren believed the brain never forgets anything.

Took Allenna to the Moulin Rouge for her 50th birthday & "showed her Paris". Because of numb diabetic feet I failed to notice that I'd skinned the sole of my right foot: raw steak. It remains a confounded nuisance 3 weeks later – a helluva time wasted at the clinic.

Eating into my week – goodbye!

Love

Stafford

(Yes – of course I know Octavio Paz!!)

On the reverse was some information about a book by George Richardson *Feedback Thought in Social Science & Systems Theory*. This was one of the few books then (and even now) to give Stafford's work some serious attention. He had given my details to the author but I never heard anything.

Brough was a man I had just bought a load of cybernetics books from, including Stafford's early books. He told me that he had worked for BEA (or was it BOAC?) in the '60s and they had Stafford advise them for a while. He had assumed that Stafford was long dead!

I had sent Stafford a volume of the Mexican poet Paz.

Cwarel Isaf 30th March 1994

My Dear David

As usual, a little peace means I'm off the multiple hooks: therefore running amuck among drafts of poems, half-done paintings, embryonic projects, pornographic excess, mathematics, images of god (do you know Vox de Nube? – Not him personally, you idiot, but the monks of Glenstal...I got up at 3.0 am & played their mad *Magnificat* twelve times in a row last night), new ways of saving civilization & sticking pins in dolls made to represent the shoddy crew in Westminster.

Therefore:

Please rush me (wotta phrase!) a Latin Ovid. The ref. I have is: Kenney, E.J. & it's Oxford 1961 or, (corrected) 1965, but any old version will do. It's *Amores & Ars Amatoria* I want NOW!!! Something's bugging me. Presume you can do this, magician, & I'd rather go to Woodstock than Broad Street. Tell me if I shouldn't. New or 2nd hand.

Congrats on the chromatic catalogue & the new literary oeuvres. Loved the piece from Finniehaddie's Awake & was going to say something clever about it. But I can't find the thing, so sorry but I decided to phone while I was in London. Did so 3 or 4 times, but you were down the pub or in orbit...

A lot is happening. Scarfe is interested in illustrating *Prang* & I've put you down for all my Wiley output (= 8, I think) around June. Meanwhile – nothing else will ever happen again if I don't stop writing bloody letters...

I do hope your new venture goes well, old friend. You appear to have embraced literary prohibition – no beer. Do you want the old Canadian edition of *DF*? Allenna brought over a dozen copies & has gone to Dublin. She'll get back here on April 1st; but that's no joke & neither is this order. As to which, the real joke is that Ovid knew the whole ludicrous story 2k years ago, isn't it?

Love

Stafford

I had now opened a shop in Woodstock, near Oxford. For my latest catalogue, tiring of alphabetical conventions, I had listed all of the books according to their colour along the spectrum (in common with Stafford, my mind has always had problems with categories). This encouraged people to study all of it – or chuck it in the bin! For some reason there were none of Stafford's books in this one.

I had sent Stafford a piece I had written in a playful Joycean (*Finnegans Wake*) style.

I found the Ovid quickly and mentioned that his *Metamorphoses* is thought to be the most influential book, in Western culture, ever published. I sent him a couple of new poems including one drawn from *Laws of Form*.

Cwarel Isaf 14th April 1994

Hello again David

Many thanks for the books & cheque herewith.

Extraordinary comment you make about *Metamorphoses*. By whhat awetorrity? (as I have heard Irish priests thunder). Preferred *Autumn Epiphany* to *An Algebra of Distinction* – not your fault. Recall that the *Algebra* ideas are over-familiar to me. Do you know my *Icons*? Ends:

'so many better emblems / could replace / these shabby icons'

– chimed with your ending.

Good about the shop. And I used to use the Bear at Woodstock every trip out to Wales in early 60s. Keep the Persian waitress in the lift for me...

You did not reply re singing monks of Glenstal, please do.

We go to London on 19th. Wed 20th – want a drink midday?! We have lunch fixed for 1.30 (sorry) & full til night, but could sure say hello (say) 11 to 1.30. Pick-up at Athenaeum. Any use? Reply soonest!

Back to *Dispute* proofs...

Love

Stafford

Publish your poems (to earn credibility for a future book) at intervals.

Stafford translated some of the Ovid and it acted as a lengthy epigraph to his collection of erotic poems *Residues of Joy* (privately circulated).

Not sure what the joke about the Persian waitress was (perhaps just as well!).

We met at the club and went on to a wine bar where Stafford and Allenna were meeting some people from the Democratic Left; this was the former Communist Party with a new name, looking for a new non-hierarchical structuring.

Cwarel Isaf 12th August 1994

Dear David

I hope that you will be pleased to know of my publisher's initiative in offering a new edition of six extant books of mine, to accompany the publication to two new books – see the leaflet.

Wiley has stoically kept five of the six books continuously in print ever since each was published – 28 years in the case of *Decision and Control*. But, as many friends have noted, the prices escalated beyond the reach of most students. The new paperback format is priced most reasonably, as you may see, especially if advantage is taken of the big reduction for the *Classic Library* set.

Of course it would be nice to hand out copies to personal friends, but it really is infeasible. Instead, Wiley has come up with a special arrangement which offers yet a further reduction to a select band. Through their courtesy I am able to write this personal letter to let you know about it.

As ever

Stafford

This was a personalised flier tucked in with something very special: a presentation copy of *Beyond Dispute: the Invention of Team Syntegrity*. I had received inscribed copies of Stafford's books before but this one had a difference – a touching mention in the acknowledgements: *Finally under this heading comes my dear friend David Whittaker, who as a bookseller in Oxford may not exactly think of himself as a sponsor of anything. His knowledge of books, and their rapid acquisition is, however, making him indispensible to a growing cluster of interdisciplinarians.*

We didn't know it then, of course, but this was to be Stafford's last book, even though he had exactly eight years left to live.

I sent Stafford a copy of the magazine *Modern Painters* which contained a long interview between David Bowie and Balthus and I suggested we could conduct something similar over a case of wine.

Cwarel Isaf 23rd November 1994

What-ho, David –

And thanks for letter & alcohol free catalogue...do you really want to be paid in Scottish pounds, or what?

Speaking of Nil, what about *Hermes*? Do you like it?

The mag is astonishing value – how can they do it?

Here's the itinerary. The London week has only mornings left. So when you suggest here (CI) in January, that'd be fine. Sooner fixed the better! So: the 'interview' plot. Well, I'm game. However, it's not very easy – it's been tried twice with me so far this year – without outcome so far. As to using Bowie/Balthus as a model...are you sure that you know ten times as much as I do? I'm prepared to have a go at being an amiable paedophile, but I can't paint that well.

My recommendation is to forget about the mag & work on the case of wine.

Flann's fun. But ould Erin...? The late T-shirt seemed to be a letter short of a slogan.

Love as ever – **Stafford**

Vanilla had published a beguiling little book *Hermes Trismegistos: Reproof of the Soul.* A collection of haiku with illustrations by her dad.

Stafford had sent a newspaper cutting about our joint hero Flann O'Brien; the 'T-shirt' is a joke term for the Irish Prime Minster (Taoiseach in Irish).

In January, on the morning I was due to drive to Wales, the country was deep in snow! Alas, the trip and the interview never came off.

Cwarel Isaf Feb. '95

Dear David

Thanks so much for the books – know Paz of course, but no, not got this definitive version: very sweet of you.

Loved the hilarious quotes! What on earth was the intention behind 'nepotism'?

"Good morning. Uncle has asked me to look into nepotism in this organisation."

I've seen my books in Blackwells – but that was years ago. Why haven't they got *Grapes* too.? You'll shortly get a letter from me/Wiley offering extra discount. You can always sell them at retail price!

Leaving tomorrow for Vanilla's; flying Monday. Back in Wales Nov/Dec.

Love – **Stafford**

I wrote a long letter to Stafford complaining about Ezra Pound. He's a writer I've always had a visceral repulsion to; I can't dissociate his personality and his fascism from his work, give me the democracy of James Joyce and Louis MacNeice any day!

The guitarist and erstwhile Eno/Bowie collaborator, Robert Fripp, had asked me to his abode to sell me some of his library (see Appendix 3).

I sent Stafford a fantastic book of literary essays, *The Geography of the Imagination*, by Guy Davenport.

The Guardian were running a series on important thinkers of the 20th century and asked readers for suggestions, I sent an enthusiastic letter about Stafford (as did quite a few people) but he never got a mention; the series appeared to be dominated by Will Hutton.

(Meanwhile the electrical firm, Rumbelows, had gone bust.)

Toronto 3rd March 1995

What-ho!

Poems arrived as was leaving Cwarel Isaf – many thanks – here's the dosh. I've spent all your time in the unlikely task of seeking to disagree with you (for once) with elegance & wit. Oh well...I always liked Ezra anyway & "Though they go mad they shall be sane". I've also liked MacNeice longer than you: *Autumn Journal*, 30s I suppose? – but not with your Irish tenacity.

Wot if Shakespeare wrote Chaucer?

V.G. about Fripp. Why's he selling? Wish he'd write to me; I'm aware of him. Given up trying to reach Eno – too old friend I guess.

Thanks a lot for doing-over *The Guardian*. Looks to me like a not-in-good-faith sales pitch for Will Hutton (I said what he's saying now in my *Dumplings* address at Queens in 1989 & the *G.* didn't even ack the MS). We'll see.

Must go. Keep the Oxford pubs from failing...

A Swansea student last year showed via VSM that Rumbelows was not a VS. He got a first.

Love

Stafford – continues...

For David the Psalmist

With whom I have shared many a song – the lesser-known verses of Christians A-Blake, egg, coupled with a jar of Tristram's Shandy and a slice of the old fruit flann – and who sent me Forty Essays forsooth by one Guy Davenport, herewith a lucid dream:

The poor old sod wrapped in assorted furs, scarves and non-thermal underwear, stomps along Bloor Street and turns into the mini-garden beside the Palmerston Library. He collapses onto a bench, drops his stick, and eruditely (for this is his adverb) mutters: 'Oh me bloody legs'. The snow is crisp, the sunlight bright, and he has Forty (Plus or Minus, to be on the safe side) Essays in his lap. Not his laptop, note – it does not exist, so it is necessary only to invent it (leave that to that techie Voltaire).

But I am digressing – as was this poor old sod. He spent the afternoon waiving the rules, not drowning in verbiage. Or so he thought, but see later. Aristotle might have described his state as a eudemonic reverie.

Upstairs in the library, a man of genuine erudition was excitedly scanning his insight. He drank in great draughts of the world's finest mild and bitter thoughts, electronically to his elbow as it were, and using the spirits of the dead white males as chasers, he verified his references at all times. Aristotle, who had difficulty in untangling the choreography of the pas-de-deux between Endorphine and Norepinephrine, might simply have called his state euphoric.

Swamped in learning, but still drinking in yet another draught, he found the bladder of his mind was fit to burst. He pulled across the slop bucket provided, and relieved the digital overload via MS/RENAL. And off he went again…zowee! The sun was declining when he found the pail was full. But it shone on still through the Windows of his Mind, and the library would not shut its gates just yet.

The old sod on the bench outside was far away when the warm stream arrived. It took him moments to collect himself – not to mention his stick. He shook off the drops of pleasing dew, and looked heavenwards for its source. There was nothing to be seen, but he seemed to hear a sort of euphoric buzzing high above. All around where he had been sitting, spring flowers were exploding through the snow. The air was fragrant too. Strange…but he stomped off homewards feeling fine.

The poor old carpet-slippered sod is handling the book. What has the Psalmist for him this time, he wonders guiltily. He opens the book at random. It is page 96: "Olson wrote 'The Kingfishers' just before going to Yucatan: in a strange economy of anticipation he wrote his meditation on the ruins before he ever saw them". Well done Olson. And so "he chose to quote" Rimbaud – in a couplet that occurs in two different poems: "Si j'ai du goût, ce n'est guères / Que pour la tetre et les pierres."

Well, if you have the taste for nothing but earth and stones it probably makes sense to say so twice, or folks might not get it. But at the bottom of the page: " Le loup criait sous les feuilles / En crachant les belles plumes / De son repas de volailles: / Comme lui je me consume."

The old sod appreciates the need to expectorate feathers after chomping up birds, but why is either this wolf or the poet eating himself as well? No wonder the wolf is moaning under the leaves – and Rimbaud is moaning all the time in any case. But Olson? Oh well.

The old sod tries again. Leafing back, he spots a parenthesis on page 51. It sticks out, self-contained: "(Remember that Ruskin accepts the Theseus of 'A Midsommer Nights Dreame' as the proper English understanding of the Athenian maze-treader.)"

As if anyone could possibly forget! The old sod is reconciled to this Guy at last, and a sentimental mist clouds the eye of his recall. It was the very first thing that he was taught when he went up to Cambridge, and no sooner did he reach Oxford as a Fellow than there it was again – scribbled on the wall of the loo in All Souls.

He must send his thanks and a heaped Benedictine to the Psalmist without delay....

Love

Stafford – 1st March 1995

I wouldn't know where to begin to comment on this inspired reverie!

Toronto 18th October 1995

My Dear David

Your cheery note on the catalogue cheered me up – I've been really worried & didn't have the heart to send you enclosed when I wrote it a month ago...

But, cheery note or not, I'm sure that something generated those bad vibes last month.

My best, in whatever case

Much love – Stafford

Virtual e-mail

To: david@dal.araidhhe

Whence this presage of downfall
of some kind?
Have you been messing with Ronan
dear my Sweeney?

I thought I saw you treed
at Glen Bolcain
shared water and watercress
and talked of women.

Now cliffs at Dunseverick:
the hag on your tail....
surely you led her on
and she is shattered?

September 1995

For the life of me I can't recall what any of this was about; interesting poem though.

But sad to say (and it does speak of downfall) this was the very last gracefully hand-written letter I was to receive from him as disaster struck two months later.

Toronto 4th July & Nil's birthday 1996

Hi there David!

As you see, I'm coming to terms with this wretched machine. For the time being, anyway, I have to accept that my handwriting is illegible.

First of all, my belated thanks for Paul Celan – profound apologies for denials. There is a very good explanation however. Checking the date of the letter that enclosed the book (now that both have been found) I can infer the likely arrival date last November. It would have been the very day that I had the stroke….Give or take a day or so, obviously, but I shoved it in a pile – and no recollection remained that I'd ever seen it. I found the thing (and many other things!) when I returned from UK and tried to catch up in May/June. Anyway, I have read it all now, and find much of it strangely attractive. I have a big problem with translations when I have no working knowledge of the original language. It strikes me as a paradox that the nearer the translator gets the less I shall understand him! This doesn't apply when I know how the language works (eg Latin). If I'm confident in the language (eg French), I begin to object to the translation! Thanks a lot, anyway.

June was a devil of a month – sunk in Colombian affairs. We have just returned from that benighted country.

Heard about Eno from Denis. What's this I read about Roger Penrose on a quantum theory of consciousness? Is this different from the *Emperor*? Have you seen Raúl's new book?

Enough for the time being I'm appallingly slow with this thing – let's try to make it print.

With love

Stafford

The 'wretched machine' in question was a voice recognition keyboard, as Stafford had lost any feeling in his fingertips for writing.

It was Stafford's 70th birthday in September and Liverpool John Moores University laid on a party. Unfortunately I couldn't make it: having done a series of book fairs I had some painful back trouble. I sent him a copy of Italo Calvino's

Six Memos for the Next Millennium. In November I went to the cottage and took him to Aberaeron for a belated birthday gourmet meal – fish and chips in the harbour. We went to a bar where he held forth to the locals in Welsh and recited his poem *Behold a Cry*, explaining to them that it used the rules of cynghanedd. We soon drank up and left! He asked my advice on what form his autobiography should take and I jokingly suggested Sterne's *Tristram Shandy* where, towards the end of 600 pages of fiendishly convoluted digressions, the eponymous hero gets born and the book ends. Stafford thought this inspired!

Over these last few years we had lengthy telephone chats but I have only scanty memories of them. The trade in letters had ended. For fifteen years Stafford had kept my postman busy.

For his 71st birthday I faxed him this 'attempted cynghanedd':

COMMUNION

To an honoured host I raise a toast and share a tune
of such exquisite variety, far from sobriety. At swim
in the grape, we swing on the vine and sing. As steersmen
we navigate warp and woof, to liberate logic
from redemptive transit through recursive requiems.
For the heart in the tabernacle, the brain of the oracle, in awe
we give thanks and live for love.

For David
... take your fair share
of happiness, my friend ...

Stafford.

APPENDICES

As the following were written on and for diverse occasions they inevitably contain some repetition:

1. **'Letter' to Stafford.**
   I read this at the memorial event for Stafford at the Royal Society of Arts, October 11, 2002.

2. **Letters to *The Guardian*.**
   I wrote the first letter to the paper the day after the obituary appeared. The second letter I wrote in response to their article about Stafford's involvement in Chile. They like to provide punning captions!

3. **Robert Fripp Letters.**
   Robert Fripp ('a small, mobile, intelligent unit') is a guitarist of international renown. He is the founder and ongoing member of the band King Crimson. He has also been involved with running J. G. Bennett's International Society for Continuous Education in Sherborne, which is based on the teachings of G. I. Gurdjieff.

4. **An Interview with Brian Eno.**
   Eno was a founder member of the highly significant band Roxy Music. He is acknowledged to be one of the finest record producers of the age and has worked with David Bowie, Talking Heads and U2, to list but a few. He invented Ambient Music ('this accommodates many levels of listening attention and is as ignorable as it is interesting'). He has had many audio/visual installations throughout the world. For over 30 years he has had a pervasive, perfusive and persuasive influence on popular culture. His article for *Studio International* is reprinted in the book:
   > *A Year with Swollen Appendices: Brian Eno's Diary*. Faber 1996
   > Select Discography:
   > *Evening Star* (1974 with Robert Fripp)
   > *Discreet Music* (1975)
   > *Another Green World* (1975)
   > *Before and After Science* (1977)
   > *Music for Airports* (1978)
   > *On Land* (1982)
   > *Thursday Afternoon* (1985)

1. 'Letter' to Stafford Beer
(please forward)

Dear Stafford,

I was so very pleased to see your picture in the paper.

But hold on old son, what's this?

Having done a double take thrice over, I realised the awful significance of the page you were featured on. Surely this must be one of those infamous *Guardian* misprints?

A gross exaggeration?

But it was, sadly, only too true.

It's a funny old business really. Your *Requiem* had predated your obituary by almost exactly 10 years.

And it really is a funny old business. We had had our last laugh together not knowing it was our last laugh together. We had raised our glasses for the last time not knowing it was to be our last synchronised swallow.

I have felt overwhelmed by so many happy and stimulating memories since our life trajectories first criss-crossed 21 years ago.

I also have stacks of wonderful entertaining letters that winged their way here from Ceredigion and Toronto, all graciously transmitted from your elegant nib.

Many of our enthusiasms chimed harmoniously, from Flann O' Brien to *Tristram Shandy*, from the liquid mathematics of Bach to Eno's ambient drones, the metrics of poetics, and of course the enlightening conundrums of Zen, Taoism and the journey to the east.

Hey! Remember that evening at Cwarel Isaf when we drank lengthy draughts of the shared illusion from the void within the glass? As the night wore on we gradually synchronised our bladders and stood, in the garden, Jimmy Riddling beneath the starry firmament discussing Plato... or was it Aristotle?

Contrast this with that afternoon in the Athenaeum, where we quaffed and gnashed our way through the wine list and menu (oh yes, that double helping of sherry trifle was rather splendid). Once again we stood in perfect accord, this time in the gentlemens' powder room, 'inspecting' the exquisite marble (none of your common porcelain here), as you held forth (in a manner of speaking) on negative entropy... or was it the reverberations of icosahedral space?

And how many grapes went into the void?

By the way, at that club of clubs how did they ever know if you were wearing a tie?

Fish and chips in Aberaeron, where you recited your fiendishly intricate cynghanedd poetry much to the affectionate bemusement of the locals.

That very first syntegration in Manchester where you unravelled your geodesic geometry and its elasticity took us all, yourself included, very much by surprise.

Stafford, it was as a dynamic event that you made your mark. An event that both informed and energised those of us lucky enough to have coincided with your transit.

You said: 'coincidence' may be the inability to see what really matters.

I wonder how many recursions of suffering are there enfolded in the metagame before the reticulum of redemption is resolved?

You described your existence as a smear of probability.

You said: each incarnation is the last.

And here we are now; your death has happened to us and within our model we endure the presence of your absent glass.

But we drank your potent brew and this has enriched our way of knowing how to know.

You said: yoga means union.

You said: there is no separation from continuous flux. This you wholly embraced as the flux embraced you.

Stafford, as a smear of probability you were far more than the sum of your masks.

Oh look here, I really must catch the last post.

I'll say my fond goodbye, and hope to catch you later in that equifinal bar.
Love and peace,
Your fellow psalmist.

P.S. You will know before I do when I am coming your way, so can you get the round in and make mine a bloody large one!

'Time' will never be called and we'll have all eternity to drain that infinite glass...

2. Letters to *The Guardian*

BEER, WINE & MUSIC BY BRIAN ENO

Dear Guardian,

I would like to add a few comments to your Stafford Beer obituary (September 4).

Beer's outstanding talents and insights were scandalously undervalued in this country. He was a true Renaissance man whose motto might well have been 'only connect'. Though he was best known for his management studies and practices, there was a far broader spectrum to his activities and achievements. He linked up cybernetic epistemology with holistic systems theory, Vedantic metaphysics and Tantric yoga. The dynamic model of non-hierarchic self-organization that he developed was applied not only to organizations and governments but also to architecture, social planning, biological systems, conflict resolution, consciousness research and even music (Brian Eno for one found it a potent compositional tool in the recording studio). His collection of essays *How Many Grapes Went Into the Wine* (1994) is a good place to start. Anyone interested in the Allende years of Chile's turbulent history will find *Brain of the Firm* (2nd ed. 1981) an essential read.

Beer was an innovative designer of his own books with different coloured pages and calligraphic diagrams among his devices for undermining habits of reading.

He was also a significant poet with one large collection *Transit* (1983) well received. As a poet Beer loved the challenge of writing in English within the constraints of diverse forms of the world's poetry, including Sanskrit and Welsh. From the latter he utilized *cynghanedd* which is a notoriously complex set of metrical rules. There is still a large body of this work unpublished.

Personally speaking (I knew him for 20 years) his generosity, patience and willingness to share were boundless. He acted as a catalyst in the synergy of ideas and people, all fuelled by much laughter and wine. Stafford Beer was a man who enriched and changed the lives of so many for the better. Unforgettable.

David Whittaker (September 5 – 2002)

CHILEAN BEER

Dear Guardian,

It was wonderful to see the account of Stafford Beer's neglected involvement with Chile at last (Santiago dreaming, September 8). Beer was a big-hearted man, who mixed notoriously well with people outside of academia, and in Chile co-wrote songs with the folk singer Angel Parra. The Chilean experience totally transformed him and in the ensuing years he offered his services to the Mexican, Uruguayan, Venezuelan and Colombian governments.

I knew him for 20 years and Chile remained uppermost in his mind. He wondered if, in fact, the very success of what he was attempting with his team hastened the demise of democracy there (as Dr Kissinger said, 'we had to save the Chilean people from themselves'). He also wrote many moving poems about Chile.

In later years his optimism never wavered, he remained busy developing a new model of participatory democracy where there is no hierarchy – no top, no bottom, no sideways – to be found in his final book *Beyond Dispute*. This had its roots in what had happened in Chile.

David Whittaker (September 9 – 2003)

3. Robert Fripp Letters

August 16th 1989

Dear Mr Whittaker,

Many thanks for your letter, and your latest news on Stafford. Just to my right is a book trough which holds what might be called "Professor Beer's Greatest Hits"; *Brain*, *Heart*, *Decision* and *Platform*. I didn't know that he was pals with Mr Bennett, although I assumed that contact was rather likely. It surprises me that Stafford isn't better known. Please let me know when the parables are available, and I would be very interested in seeing the paintings, whenever they might surface. If you are ever in touch with him, please give him my best wishes. I once wrote to him, and he very generously replied.

Best wishes,

Robert Fripp

May 18th 1990

Dear David,

I don't use cybernetic thinking as such in musical work. Music is its own language. But, if one examined the principles of operation they would be exactly the same with different terminology. Eno doesn't have a facility in musical language, although he has a background of procedure in the fine arts and good taste. This serves him far better than most musicians I know, although it does limit his executive action. Hence the collaborations. I do use Bennett's Systematics as a tool in thinking, and two friends of mine in Washington have recently also been working on the icosahedron as a way of presenting the 48 triads (World 48 in Mr Gurdjieff's terminology). Very few people are able to see into the world of metaphysics on more than an intellectual level. One of these two people does, and it's quite refreshing to be near a creative mind. This is my interest in Stafford: his act of seeing is more important to me than what he sees. In a sense, the act of seeing is the seeing. So, I remain a Beer fan too! Envy, envy of your four days.

Best wishes,

Robert

4. AN INVERVIEW WITH BRIAN ENO

DW Stafford's books and cybernetics – which came first?

BE Cybernetics very early on, because I was at an art school where we had a cybernetician as one of the tutors (Ipswich '64–'66). This was a very unusual thing in an art school then, but the principal of the school was Roy Ascott who was very interested in cybernetics and thought that this was the science that artists ought to be aware of, it was the science of now, just like people might say that complexity theory is the science of this point in time. He'd studied with W. Ross Ashby, in fact I think we had Ashby come and lecture once. So I already was alert to that body of thinking and it very much fitted in with what became the dominant philosophy of that art school which was process not product. The idea became that artists should concentrate on the way they were doing things, not just the little picture that came out at the end, and the picture was even relegated to the status of a memento of the process: the process was the interesting part of the work. This has become a mainstay of Brit. Art which is why it often looks so bloody old fashioned to me. It often looks like what we were doing in the '60s, especially the more conceptual stuff. Anyway I shouldn't be too haughty!

DW Duchamp did it about 90 years ago

BE Yes, there's that as well. Anyway, I had this cybernetic thing in my mind and was very interested in that body of ideas, and in 1974 my mother-in-law, with whom I had a very good intellectual friendship (in fact we're still friends), said she'd got a book from Swiss Cottage library which I might like. It was called *Brain of the Firm* and it was the first I'd heard of Stafford and I was very, very impressed by it. I can still remember chunks of it verbatim. Then in 1975 I wrote an essay, round about the same time I was starting to do lectures and talks, in which I quoted from Stafford's book quite extensively. People were quite baffled by what I was saying. I've met people since who went to those lectures who tell me they had absolutely no idea what I was talking about or why I was bothering to do it. It's often been the reaction: 'why bother?'. I originally wrote that essay for the *Studio* and I sent a copy to Stafford. I said 'I'm sorry to do this and I've never done it before but I really like your work and thought you might be interested in an unusual application of it. You don't have to reply it's just for your own information'. He sent a letter back that said 'Would that one hundredth of the letters I receive were one tenth as interesting'! He also said 'I'm in London next week can I come and see you?', which he did. He came to my place in Maida Vale, this big hairy guy arrived.

DW   This was 1975 when he was moving to his solitude in Wales?

BE   That's right. It was very smoky, he was smoking a lot and drinking sherry, he came with a bottle of sherry and his cigars and stayed quite a long time, about 4 hours. I remember we talked about what had happened in Chile, I was interested in that and he told me the inside story of how things had gone there and talked about new forms of governance and what governments would have to be like in the future. None of that has come true yet!

DW   Different forms of hierarchy?

BE   And different responsiveness, different ways of making decisions and absorbing information. How do you get the right feedback, basically; how do you filter it – governments are obviously swamped in stuff; how to make longer term decisions? Governments have to be thinking many years ahead but they very rarely are.

DW   Almost 30 years later here you are with 'The Clock of the Long Now'.

BE   Yes. So Stafford left and the house took quite a long time to defumigate! I stayed in touch with him then and we wrote to each other often. I didn't see him again until 1977 when he invited me to visit him in Wales. I've forgotten the name of the place…

DW   Cwarel Isaf, which means lowest quarry.

BE   It certainly was.

DW   There's now a Cwarel Isaf Institute of Management in Switzerland. It's named after a Welsh quarry!

BE   In honour of an English man. The idea was I was going there to stay for a couple of days. I actually put on some quite smart clothes and it was a filthy day, absolutely filthy, wet, muddy day the kind of weather I always associate with Wales! I got the taxi to take me there and as I walked down the muddy lane these four dogs ran out at me, they were like huge mud paint brushes and they just went *FFLOPFF!* like that (gives graphic demonstration of being mauled and wrestled to the ground). I was instantly covered in mud; it was awful! I was staying just over night so I hadn't brought a change of clothes, you know. Stafford didn't seem to notice this had happened and said he was very happy to see me and we started in talking straight away. There was no 'how was your journey' or anything like that. He said he'd been working on the theory of closure and started drawing diagrams and showing me equations. The cottage was very sort of bachelor, I thought. He was smoking away his cigars, there was smoke everywhere I could hardly see him.

DW   And his fire generated more smoke.

BE   Exactly, he was drinking the sherry all of the time, but there was no sense I had that he was not in control of himself at all. Was he still a sherry drinker when you knew him?

DW   Wine and water was always on the go, but it didn't seem to affect him and he worked late into the night.

BE   He was very energetic. That day I arrived around lunch time and hadn't had any lunch, so I was quite hungry but there was no food forthcoming. The talk was very intense and about four or five o' clock in the afternoon I said 'you don't have anything to eat do you?' He said 'Oh, I'm sorry I should have offered' and he got some potatoes, put them in a pot with some water and put them on a very low gas. They were sitting there for hours and hours, there was moisture coming from them adding to the general fug in the room. There was steam coming from the pots, his cigars, the fire, the general humidity of that day and my stomach was going and going. Eventually I said 'I am so hungry I've got to eat something'; the potatoes were eventually dished up with nothing else – it was just potatoes.

During this conversation he said 'I carry a torch, a torch that was handed to me along a chain from Ross Ashby, it was handed to him from..', not Wiener, who was the American guy...

DW   Warren McCulloch?

BE   Yes, McCulloch. He was telling me the story of the lineage of this idea, this body of ideas and said 'I want to hand it to you, I know it's a responsibility and you don't have to accept, I just want you to think about it'. It was a very strange moment for me, it was a sort of religious initiation of some kind and I didn't feel comfortable about it somehow. I said 'Well, I'm flattered that you think that but I don't see how I can accept it without deciding to give up the work I do now and I would have to think very hard about that'. We left it saying the offer is there, but it was very strange, we never referred to it again, I wasn't in touch with him that much after that. I'm sure it was meant with the best of intentions and so on but it was slightly weird.

DW   You did see him later at his Toronto home. He told me that you wired up a kind of ambient system in his apartment.

BE Yes, I remember Allenna was there too. I also lived in Toronto for a little while, 1983 I think.

DW Stafford's ideas, particularly in the 1970s, became integrated into your studio work.

BE It's one of the most important bodies of theory in my life, it's still a very underexploited and underecognised body of work. I'm sure that sooner or later people are going to say 'Yes, this is were it started, this was the person who first articulated this', it's very current to me.

DW Is it still relevant?

BE Yes, I'm now quite interested in complexity theory and various forms of self-generating systems, autocatalysis and all those sorts of things and they're all prefigured in that book.

DW Even back in the '50s he was getting on for all this stuff, but because it's been compartmentalised under management text books it hasn't become a broader seller like the chaos, complexity books. Most people don't look in the management section of book stores, they aren't very sexy!

BE No, there aren't that many great books in that area.

DW *Brain of the Firm*, which was published by Allen Lane, was due to come out in Penguin paperback. Remember those black ones? They had von Bertalanffy, Marcuse, Levi-Strauss, all cutting edge thinking. But there was a sudden major change of policy and it just failed to appear. It would have circulated Stafford's name and ideas far more widely.

BE I'm sure that would have made a big difference, I mean if my mother-in-law hadn't been looking through the library I don't think I'd ever have heard of him, or at least not for a long, long time. That was a pure piece of luck. I didn't know anybody else who'd ever heard of him. It was completely out of the blue; certainly I would never have looked in the management section.

DW Were there any other musicians who picked up on him? I know Fripp admires him.

BE Fripp heard about him from me I think.

DW Even Bowie lists *Brain* as a desert island book, so Stafford told me.

BE He heard it from me as well, I didn't know any other musicians.

DW You've single-handedly boosted his sales, you've been his only salesman!

BE I can't think of any other people who were even interested in that area, let alone him in particular, or who were interested in thinking about music in that kind of way. That essay I wrote still represents, to most people, a very obscure way to think about music.

DW There were a few classical boffins, Xenakis perhaps, but they're difficult people to listen to, who got into the mathematics of cybernetics.

BE In a way the mathematics is not the interesting part for me, the interesting part is how you rethink how something is made, how something comes into being. Even with the composers you mention, they were quite classical composers because in the end they wrote it all out; in a sense they described it in advance. Now there were other people like Cornelius Cardew, John Cage, Christian Wolff who were doing something more interesting, they were inventing systems which produced music. Now, that's a total break from the Western classical idea. The idea is that your job as a composer is to design a machine or system which you can provide inputs to and which will output music. So you forego the thing that composers usually do which is to design music in detail, so that you're no longer exactly the architect of a piece of work but more the designer of a musical ecosystem. You put a few things in place and see how they react or what they do to each other.

Anyway, the phrase that probably crystallised it that I quoted in that essay says 'instead of specifying it in full detail you specify it only somewhat, you then ride on the dynamics of the system in the direction that you want to go'. That really became my idea of a working method.

DW You have often quoted Stafford's distinction between heuristics and algorithms – were there other important notions of Stafford's that you applied in the studio?

BE Well, it so fundamentally changed the way that I thought about music that it's very difficult to translate it into individual things, it just changed the whole way I worked. Most of the things I do now have something to do with that body of ideas and of course when you find a writer who's saying something you really want to hear it's because you were getting there yourself anyway. I had a lot of ideas in place, but this is were they were articulated. For example a very important influence on me were those early Steve Reich pieces and they demanded explanation of some kind and the Cardew piece *The Great Learning*, which completely fascinated me. There were no art writers talking about those things in any way I thought interesting at all and actually I still think there aren't. If I read art writers now I think they're using entirely the wrong language, they don't say anything that tells me anything I want to know about the work. In fact it's possibly the worst form of socially sanctioned writing going! It's possible for people to write for people, not other academics, and to say things that make sense. The arrogance of the art writers is first of all 'You wouldn't understand it anyway' and two, 'I can bluff it, nobody's going to notice'! I think it is mostly bluff writing really.

DW In a way you were applying management to managing other musicians?

BE That's true. I never thought of it like that, as management.

DW Would you say there is an album from that period which is a particular Staffordian album?

BE Actually everything I did from 1975 was to some extent informed by him. *Music for Airports* is a pure example of a systems record: set a few things in motion and record the result.

DW No dissonance in there?

BE It depends what you feed into the system. Now this is an interesting point because in the sort of classic 'process not product' school that I came from, your job as an artist was to design the system: that was the beauty of the work, you put anything into it and didn't mind what came out. I detected a bit of this in Reich. I remember getting into a big public argument in New York at a symposium in 1978, when the panel included John Rockwell, music critic of *The New York Times*, and Philip Glass. I said I felt that the success of Reich's work was that it was a brilliantly economical and intelligent way to make music. I then talked about the failure of it. Any musician who listened to the results of what they were doing would not use those instruments. This was after the early tape pieces when he was using those dreadful orchestral percussion things, tam-tams and so on, they sounded so diagrammatic that what they seemed to be saying was 'Listen to my system' not 'Listen to my music' and I said it was weak and arty to do that: you can have the system and you can have the music as well. This prompted total outrage that I, a pop musician, had the temerity to criticise Reich! A famous critic came up afterwards and said 'what have you ever done for music that you can talk like that?' It's such an art thing: 'He's questioned the orthodoxy'. Whenever somebody asks what right does someone have, you know they're in the wrong somehow. That's a question that belies a call to authority that doesn't deserve to be evoked. Anyhow, one of the things I quote from that little phrase from Stafford was the last bit 'in the direction you want to go', it's not just you ride on the dynamics of the system, full stop. Which was what was happening in the art stuff that was edging towards that, it said 'hey, whatever happens happens'. I thought I wanted to make something that I would like to hear as well, I don't only want to be intrigued by the system.

DW This calls for judgement.

BE Exactly, and trust the fact that you can make judgements. They might not be the same as everyone else's and they might not be eternally valid or whatever, but for Christ's sake I make them all the time about other things, why shouldn't I make them about my own work? So I wanted the Staffordian approach to do two things: to pitch me into aesthetic areas beyond where my taste would naturally take me. That's one of the things you find working with systems, that they throw up configurations that you couldn't have thought of, I wanted the system to confront me with novelty; but I did also want to say 'I prefer this part of it to that part, this part doesn't make sense, that part does'. So I didn't think as my critics at the conference did, to want to impose that making my own judgements was a step back into kitsch or it wasn't rigorous enough. I thought you're not being rigorous. If the thing doesn't work that's a lack of rigor: rigor is when you test the conceptualisation of something against the realisation of it. Rigor is bringing those two together and saying 'well if that realisation doesn't work maybe I should be looking at this conceptualisation again'.

DW Bateson talked about getting a balance between rigor and imagination.

BE Yes, that's right and what I call the systemic approach to working is certainly very good at imagination expanding. Another thing that happened on *Airports* was something that only I would know about, it was internal to the workings of the record. The first piece on the second side (I'm talking about vinyl here because it was very important to me that it was a two sided record) used piano and voices and did exactly the same as the pure voice piece (second track of first side), which had a number of loops and they reconfigured, but what I did in that side *2/1*, I listened to it as a long sequence of music, and thought this section here actually interests me more than the rest of it, it seems to have a melodic shape or structure to it. I then took that section out and redid the looping process with that. I had this word in my mind at the time called 'chunking-up'. I had the idea that I wanted these pieces to evolve somehow so I didn't just want to put into place systems that spat out material and leave it there. I wanted there to be a way of saying that this cluster, this sequence, this four minutes or whatever is something special going on, so let's use that as our raw material input. Next we do a system where we don't keep going back to atoms; let's start with whole cells now and then let it evolve.

DW You've been acknowledged as a major influence on the last 30 years of popular music and culture and I wonder if Stafford hadn't existed would all of this history be quite different?

BE That's an interesting thought.

DW As a management man he's had this significant side effect channelled through you.

BE Yes, this does happen sometimes. Something burrows in from another field like an invading seed. But, yes I think it would be different, I had a lot of confidence because of the articulacy with which he stated those ideas, they were ideas I was getting to myself anyway, but because there was suddenly a way of really thinking about them and telling them to other people it made them clearer to myself. I was very, very confident about them. It didn't even seem controversial to me at all. I think those records like *Discreet Music* and *Music for Airports*, which are very austere in a way, they're very unornamented and they are what they are, there's no attempt to make anyone like them. Because they were like that they were clearly a newly articulated position in pop music. That's what made them different from say *Tubular Bells*, that had some of the same ideas, but it was so obviously out to appeal that it hid what was interesting about itself. *Tubular Bells* would never have become the sort of manifesto that those early Ambient records did become; they did have a sort of manifesto status. It was very clear that they stood for something, they were the embodiment of some idea and people talked about them a lot as a result. I think they became a sort of standard for something that hadn't been officially permitted in pop before. At least they provided licence for people to do something, to think in a certain way or to think at all. At another level they gave people something to think about which was how do we do things, how do we make things and bring things into being. That's very much to do with the confidence I felt from having him behind me as it were. Because that's what it felt like, I didn't feel that I'd invented all of this. I felt that I could see deep roots going in lots of directions in the fine art world and in the science world of which Stafford was a part. It all seemed very clear to me, very strong, I didn't have to apologise for it.

DW Cybernetics itself, a much abused word now. From cybergasms to cybershamans, that magical word has got a bit lost. Do you have a reply when people ask you what is cybernetics?

BE I always say to people I think it's the attempt to understand how systems work and then if they say 'what do you mean?', I say systems that are not stationary, that are living in the world and circulate information around themselves and correspond with the rest of the world as well. Cybernetics is how those processes happen, you know, how does a creature's impact on the rest of the world reflect back to its actions, for example how does it watch what it's doing and how does it change what it's doing in relation to its effect and so on.

DW Circular causality was a big discovery of cybernetics.

BE That's right.

DW Stafford also commissioned you to write another paper, *Self-Organization and Autopoiesis in Modern Music*.

BE I wrote it, funnily enough, on my thirtieth birthday in New York, May 15 1978. I can remember very clearly. I had done a lot of work for it, but I wrote the final draught all on that day, I spent the whole day doing it. It was a very good piece: a kind of an update and amplification of the *Studio* essay. I don't know where it is now, I haven't got a copy of it.

DW I asked you, about 10 years ago, for it and you promised to dig it out. Are you now telling me you've lost this masterpiece from your thirtieth birthday?

BE Stafford had a copy, I sent it to him. I have so much stuff here, I came across a letter from Cage the other day, written to me when I was 19 or 20.

DW You've also referred to Fuller's *Synergetics*.

BE He wasn't relevant in much detail to tell the truth. I liked him as a figure and as a presence. In terms of specifics I don't recall anything that I learned from him. Just the general approach seemed nice.

DW In the '70s Peter Schmidt was also very important to you. I have the old catalogue *Cybernetic Serendipity* from that famous 1968 ICA show.

BE He and Jaschia Reichhardt were the curators. I don't know how it got that title, that's the way the art world works. They try to find a word that people seem to be saying and think 'that's probably what we're doing'. It was quite an interesting show, very mixed up with lots of different things. Gustav Metzger was in there, who I bumped into only a few days ago. He was the father of and the only proponent as far as I know of auto-destructive art.

DW But Schmidt became a guiding light?

BE He was an artist who liked thinking analytically about what he was doing. I can't tell you how rare this is! I've spent a life being lonely as an artist. I don't know many other artists who think about what they're doing in the sense of wanting to pick it apart.

DW Yet they all have something to say.

BE They've all got something to say, but it's not very interesting by and large. They all seem to stand slightly in awe of their own talent. What I liked about Peter was he wanted to worry it; he wanted to find out why he wanted to do it, why it worked, why this didn't work. It seems to me so many artists live in fear of bursting their bubble; they've a basic lack of confidence about what they're doing and they daren't question it too much in case they can't do it anymore. Like the centipede who starts counting its feet as it's walking. I really liked Peter because I had this very long conversation going on for 10 years with him about how to do it and why to do it. That's also important, the one question that artists never ask is 'What's it for?'. They might talk about all sorts of other things, but you never hear two artists sitting and asking 'Why are we doing this?'. Again, it's a question you don't ask. Where does it fit in society, what does it do for people, why do people like it, could they do without it? All those sort of questions.

DW They'd say that they have an urge to do it.

BE I would say why? It's a difficult thing for me, I have a lot of friends who are scientists and it's not because I want to be a scientist – it's because I can have conversations with them at a level that I want to have conversations. I find with artists that isn't happening. There's a history of inarticulacy, at least, I would say, for the last 50, 60, 70 years. There's not a history of a public language and critics have completely failed to provide any kind of way of talking about what artists are doing now. When you had craft to talk about there was something to talk about, OK not very interesting, but now that clearly isn't an issue.

DW Duchamp was particularly erudite.

BE Cage was very erudite as well. But the number of artists who have been is so small that they stand out, whereas if you turn to science there are many, many, many scientists who are very able to talk about what they're doing. I always say to people if you ask twenty scientists what's science for, they'll come up with pretty similar answers: 'we want to find out how things fit together' or some sort of version of that. If you ask twenty artists what's art for, I'll bet not two of them will agree. They would even question the validity of the question.

DW Have you read some other cyberneticians like Bateson, Maturana, Varela?

BE The funny thing is I'm a very peculiar student in a way: I don't need many instances of something. For example, nearly everything I've understood about funk music has been from listening to one record really, but I've listened to it so many times and so closely and that's been the history of my life really. Although I have all these books here, the number that I've read with real depth and attention is very small. I skim through them all mainly to find if they're going to be books that I can do that with. There are very few in my life that have done it for me. There's John Cage's *Silence*, I still have my original version there, I must have read it thirty times probably. As I reread it, it kept changing as my context changed. I'm the opposite of a sightseer in that respect, I don't want to see everything. I really want to go into a few things and Stafford for me was the doorway into a whole way of thinking. I read *Brain* closely, over and over. Yes, I did read those authors you mentioned. Autopoiesis was a new word but the concept was prefigured here in Stafford I felt, so it didn't strike me as 'Wow, it's amazing!', it was just 'Oh, there's a word for it, a word for this thing we've been thinking about'. It wasn't until cellular automata and complexity theory started appearing that I felt there was something a step on from Stafford. *Decision and Control* and *Platform for Change* are also very good.

Eno – 'a drifting clarifier'

SUBSCRIBERS

Denis Adams – Mold, Wales
Rhodri Asby – Cardiff, Wales
Robin Asby – Todmorden, Yorkshire
Graham Barnes – Stockholm, Sweden
Ian Bolton – Greenwich, London
Jac Christis – Nijmegen, Netherlands
Toby Cornish – Berlin, Germany
Ursula & James Cornish – Camden, London
David Alban Davies – Chipping Norton, Oxon
Rupert Dodds – Charlbury, Oxon
Gail Doran – Netley Abbey, Hampshire
Kevin Eden – Edgley, Stockport
Peter & Budge English – Ruthin, Wales
Raúl Espejo – Lincoln
Angela Espinosa – Scarborough, Yorkshire
Ed Fenton – Charlbury, Oxon
Robert Fripp – nr Salisbury, Wiltshire
Clive Gibson-Leitch – Charlbury, Oxon
Ranulph Glanville – Southsea, Hampshire
Margaret Godel & David Homewood – Charlbury, Oxon
Becca Harris-Clark – Denmead, Hampshire
Doug Haynes – Liverpool
Trevor Hilder – Trowbridge, Wiltshire
Kerry Hodgson – Madrid, Spain
David Howard – Chislehurst, Kent
Dave 'Jake' Jacobs – Battersea, London
David Tom & Llinas Jones – Lampeter, Wales
Gareth Jones – nr Lampeter, Wales
Hans Losscher – Amerongen, Netherlands
Tony Mann – Lewisham, London
Penny Marrington – Todmorden, Yorkshire
Martin Maw – Charlbury, Oxon
Ray Miles – Beckenham
John Oldham – Ramsden, Oxon
Adrian Peacock – Richmond, London
Edward Richardson – Cumnor, Oxon
Toby Ridge – Winchester, Hampshire
Markus Schwaninger – St Gallen, Switzerland
Neville Shack – Kensington, London
Peter Stadelmann – Glottbrugg, Switzerland
Anthony Stark – Denmead, Hampshire
Sarah Stoten – Shipston-on-Stour, Warwickshire
Joe Truss – Ontario, Canada
Alan Ward – Wadham College, Oxford
David Weir – nr Nice, France
Simon Whitehead – Charlbury, Oxon
David Kim Whittaker – St Ives, Cornwall